PRAGUE

Compact Guide: Prague is the ultimate quick-reference guide to this glorious city. It tells you all you need to know about Prague's attractions, from the Castle to the Lesser Quarter and the Charles Bridge to the Old Town Square, from the city's wealth of art and architecture to its hotels, restaurants and inviting taverns.

This is one of 133 Compact Guides, combining the interests and enthusiasms of two of the world's best-known information providers: Insight Guides, whose innovative titles have set the standard for visual travel guides since 1970, and Discovery Channel, the world's premier source of nonfiction television programming.

Part of the Langenscheidt Publishing Group

Insight Compact Guide: Prague

Written by: Horst Becker
English version: Jane Michael and Pam Barrett
Photography: Glyn Genin
Additional photography: Mark Read; Phil Wood; AKG London
    (p 43T/B); Bodo Bondzio (p 108); Polfoto Martin Zakora/
    Topham Picturepoint (p 12)
Cover picture: David Noton/Taxi/Getty Images
Designed and updated by: Maria Lord
Picture Editor: Hilary Genin
Cartographic Editor: Maria Donnelly

Editorial Director: Brian Bell
Managing Editor: Tony Halliday

CONTACTING THE EDITORS: As every effort is made to provide accurate information in this publication, we would appreciate it if readers would call our attention to any errors and omissions by contacting:
Apa Publications, PO Box 7910, London SE1 1WE, England.
Fax: (44 20) 7403 0290
e-mail: insight@apaguide.co.uk

Information has been obtained from sources believed to be reliable, but its accuracy and completeness, and the opinions based thereon, are not guaranteed.

© 2005 APA Publications GmbH & Co. Verlag KG Singapore Branch, Singapore.

First Edition 1995, Second Edition 2002, Updated 2004, Revised 2005
Printed in Singapore by Insight Print Services (Pte) Ltd
Original edition © Polyglott-Verlag Dr Bolte KG, Munich

Distributed in the UK & Ireland by:
GeoCenter International Ltd
The Viables Centre, Harrow Way, Basingstoke,
Hampshire RG22 4BJ
Tel: (44 1256) 817 987, Fax: (44 1256) 817 988

Distributed in the United States by:
Langenscheidt Publishers, Inc.
36-36 33rd Street 4th Floor, Long Island City, NY 11106
Tel: (1 718) 784 0055, Fax: (1 718) 784 0640

Worldwide distribution enquiries:
APA Publications GmbH & Co. Verlag KG (Singapore Branch)
38 Joo Koon Road, Singapore 628990
Tel: (65) 6865 1600, Fax: (65) 6861 6438

www.insightguides.com

Introduction

Places

Culture

Travel Tips

▷ **Jewish Quarter (p70)** The cemetery and a cluster of synagogues testify to Prague's once vibrant Jewish community.

◁ **Teyn Church (p65)** Dominating the Old Town with its twin towers, this church is one of the city's landmarks.

▽ **St Vitus (p23)** Prague's Gothic cathedral contains not only chapels and tombs, but also some fine stained glass, including this window designed by art nouveau artist Alphons Mucha.

◁ **Astronomical Clock (p63)** This intriguing device is one of Prague's most famous symbols.

△ **National Gallery (p42)** Housed in the Sternberg Palace, the Gallery's Old Masters collection includes some outstanding paintings.

△ **Prague Castle (p18)** With its commanding position above the river, the Castle has been key to every epoch in the city's history. The Cathedral, the Royal Palace and many other monuments are contained within its walls.

△ **Charles Bridge (p57)** Spanning the Vltava River, the bridge is a Gothic masterpiece, with the added impact of some fine baroque sculpture.

▷ **National Theatre (p84)** The city's main cultural venue and potent symbol of the Czech spirit.

▽ **Loreto Church (p45)** A famous pilgrimage church with a copy of Bramante's Casa Santa and frescoed cloisters.

◁ **Wenceslas Square (p81)** Dominated at its top end by the National Museum and this fine equestrian statue of St Wenceslas (Prague's patron saint), and flanked by some magnificent art nouveau buildings, this is the bustling focal point of the New Town.

The Golden City

Even the moon assured the great Czech writer Jan Neruda that 'no other city can compare with the beauty of Prague', whilst for Paul Valéry there was 'no other place in the world where the magnificence of the whole is subordinated to so many precious details and cameos'. Virtually no other city has been praised across the centuries so continuously and effusively. 'Prague the Golden' and 'Prague of the Hundred Towers' are just two of its descriptions, which seem as fitting now as they were in days long past.

Anybody who gazes over the city from the parapets of Hradčany Castle must surely appreciate why. Prague is the most fortunate of all European cities; fortunate because its skyline was never touched by the ravages of war, and because its essential appearance was never scarred by the addition of modern eyesores. Viewed from Castle Hill, the historical centre, whose hundreds of rooftops reflect the golden patina of the midday sun, clings to the gently curving bend in the River Vltava (also called the Moldau). Its banks seem to be only just held together by the filigreed constructions of its bridges: on the one side lies the Lesser Quarter and on the other the Old Town.

Opposite: golden façades – a view of the Lesser Quarter Bridge Tower
Below: the Astronomical Clock at the Old Town Hall – an icon of Prague

LOCATION AND SIZE

Prague/Praha, the capital of the Czech Republic, is situated on the River Vltava, spread out between seven hills. It lies 176–397m (575–1,300 ft) above sea level, at 50° North and 14° East; about the same latitude as Frankfurt, Land's End and Vancouver. The city has a population of 1.3 million living over a total area of 497 sq km (190 sq miles). Historic Prague boasts over 500 towers and steeples, and the city's parks and gardens cover a total area of 870 hectares (2,150 acres).

It is not difficult to find your bearings in Prague, especially as the most important sights can be reached on foot. The city's

CLIMATE CHART

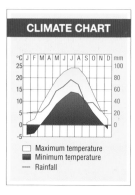

☐ Maximum temperature
■ Minimum temperature
--- Rainfall

small centre (Prague 1) is divided into the historic quarters of Malá Strana (Lesser Quarter), Staré Město (Old Town), and Nové Město (New Town). The latter is centred around Wenceslas Square and extends to a street called Na příkopě. Adjacent and to the north is the Staré Město, which extends across the Old Town Square (Staroměstské náměstí) and the right bank of the Vltava and the Charles Bridge. The picturesque Malá Strana lies on the left of the river. Two other self-contained districts are the Josefov (Jewish Quarter) and Hradčany, the Castle Quarter.

CLIMATE

Prague's climate is characterised by fairly mild winters and moderately warm summers. From a climatic point of view, the best times to visit Prague are the spring and autumn. May, when the parks and gardens are in full bloom, heralds the classic music festival, Prague Spring, while the mild autumn with its stable weather offers the best prospects for extended strolls around town.

Art nouveau sculptures on the Hlalol Choir Building on Masarykovo nábřeží

THE CZECH REPUBLIC

Prague is the seat of the national president and the National Assembly of the Czech Republic. On 1 January 1993 the federal state of Czechoslovakia ceased to exist. The revolution which swept the country in 1989 brought the old quarrels between the two republics once again to the forefront, and strong political movements in both republics negotiated the division of the country during the course of 1992.

The Czech Republic opted to go for more rapid change, under a programme of economic reforms based on the principle of the free market. Although the privatisation process was marked by corruption, the current government has taken huge steps toward integration with the West. The country joined NATO in 1998, and became a full member of the European Union in 2004.

The population of the republic is more than 10 million, and while the majority are ethnic

Czechs, there remain sizeable German and Romany (Gypsy) minorities.

INDUSTRY AND TRADE

Czech industry has made great progress since World War II, particularly in the spheres of mechanical engineering and iron and steel production. Approximately 10 percent of industry is centred in and around the capital. Apart from these three major industries, the Czech Republic also manufactures textiles, shoes, wood products and glass, for which Bohemia has always been renowned. The mechanical engineering industry is heavily export-oriented; the major markets are in eastern and southeastern Europe.

Joint ventures with foreign companies have been permitted since 1988, and many of these are now flourishing. Following the Velvet Revolution, Prague has been flooded with foreign investment, and while some of the old domestic industries are floundering, many multinational corporations maintain offices in the city.

HEART OF THE EMPIRE

Princess Libuše, the mythical founder of Prague, had a vision of a city 'whose glory will reach to the stars'. Though thankfully free of skyscrapers,

The Vltava
Overwhelmed by the beauty of Prague's architecture, it's easy to overlook one of the city's best features: the Vltava river itself, winding in a graceful S-shape through the heart of the city. Known as the Moldau by some, its beauty has inspired writers and musicians for centuries – not least Bedřich Smetana, whose symphonic poem named for the river celebrates its long passage through the Czech lands, culminating in the grand sweep through Prague.

Below: a city tram
Bottom: the Lesser Quarter, Charles Bridge and Old Town

there is little doubt that Prague was destined for greatness from its very conception.

Prague's position at the geographical heart of Europe has made it a focal point for much of the continent's history; both its high points and its tragic lows. Art, music and religious movements all owe much to this tiny city that developed excellent centres of learning, and which managed to make its mark despite spending much of its history under foreign domination.

Much of the credit is due to Charles IV. When he was crowned Holy Roman Emperor in 1355, the city became the capital of all Europe, and under his enlightened leadership blossomed for the first time into a true metropolis.

DEFENESTRATION – A LOCAL TRADITION

Things were not always peaceful in Prague. When Hussite reformers, railing against endemic corruption in the Catholic Chuch, threw members of the King's Council out the window of the New Town Hall in the First Defenestration of Prague in 1419, the ensuing Hussite wars radically altered the status quo on the Continent and laid the groundwork for Martin Luther's reforms. And then in 1618, when Protestant Czech lords threw two governors of Bohemia out of Hradčany's Council Room window in the Second Defenestration, Europe again followed Prague's lead, and the bloody Thirty Years' War was set in motion.

CZECHS, GERMANS AND JEWS

Under the Habsburgs, the city flourished as the occasional capital of the Empire, growing into a vibrant amalgamation of Czech, German and Jewish culture. The relationship wasn't always easy, but out of the combination came some of the greatest artistic achivements, scientific innovations and architectural wonders of Europe. Johann Kepler's innovations in physical astronomy, Franz Kafka's writings and Antonín Dvořák's symphonies: all were inspired by the atmosphere, and the people, of Prague.

Libuše

The foundation of Prague is surrounded by myth. According to legend, Princess Libuše, ruler of a Slavic tribe which had always been led by women, chose a humble ploughman, Přemysl, as her husband. She instructed him to seek out a village on the banks of the Vltava and to found a city there, for which she prophesied great things. Přemysl led a group of followers to the place Libuše described and there founded the Golden City of Prague.

Franz Kafka

INDEPENDENCE AND REVOLUTION

The city's true glory days were under the first
Czechoslovak Republic. Autonomous for the first
time in three centuries, Prague suddenly found
itself the richest city in Europe after the devastation World War I had wrought elsewhere. It was
a high time for Praguers, and they celebrated in
true form by erecting many of the grand buildings, broad boulevards and lively cafés that still
grace the city today.

Now, some 15 years after the Velvet Revolution, Prague is entering a new era of prosperity.
Not content to rely on the tourist industry for a
living, Praguers are celebrating their new-found
freedom by branching out once again – not only
in traditional areas such as art and music, but also
technology and international trade. As Prague
lives out its third millennium, Libuše's prophecy
continues to be fulfilled.

*Below: passageway to the
National Gallery
Bottom: the National Theatre*

THE CITY TODAY

Though neon signs may glare along the boulevards of Prague today, the city's old magic
remains strong. Chances are that just a few steps
away, on a quiet side street, the stones will speak
to you of the times when Rabbi Loew's legendary
creation, the Golem, protected the Jewish Quarter; when kings marched down the Royal Way

to their coronations; when traders from afar sold their treasures in the markets, and revolutions brewed out of whispers in the streets.

When the last revolution swept across Europe, bringing the fall of the Iron Curtain in 1989, Prague was once again opened up to the Western world, and although Czechs were initially a bit overwhelmed by the attention their city drew, there now exists a comfortable rapport between locals and foreigners.

The Velvet Revolution
On November 17, 1989, a relatively peaceful student march through Prague became a full-blown march, and police responded violently. Thousands gathered on Wenceslas Square to protest, jingling their keys in the air and demanding democracy after 40 years of communist party rule. When the regime resigned the next day, the calmest revolution in European history was accomplished. Though many Soviet-era officials remain in positions of power, the nation has since made remarkable strides in putting the past behind it. If only every revolution could be accomplished so easily.

FOREIGN RESIDENTS

Immediately after the Velvet Revolution, thousands of Westerners – many of them young Americans – came to live in the city. Drawn by the adventure of living in a post-communist country, as well as by the relatively low cost of living, they taught English, held art exhibitions and open-mike poetry readings, started businesses, and generally revelled in a kind of freedom not often found in the West.

As Prague's economy evolved into full-blown capitalism, however, much of the initial charm that drew these young 'Bohemians' began to wane, and there was a sort of exodus in the mid-1990s. But many who had intermarried with locals or found a comfortable niche stayed, and there remains a sizable expatriate population in the city – although these days the expats are analysts and bankers not students and poets.

The Lesser Quarter under water

FLOODING

In 2002 a series of floods occurred across Central Europe. One of the worst affected cities was Prague, where the Vltava burst its banks, overwhelming the defences hurriedly put in place to protect the city's monuments. The low lying areas were inundated, with the Lesser Quarter, Kampa Island and the Jewish Quarter suffering damage. Although these were the worst floods in the city for over 100 years, and the bill for the clean-up and restoration has run into millions of euros, there is now little evidence of the devastation.

HISTORICAL HIGHLIGHTS

Prehistoric Evidence of Stone Age habitation around Prague.

circa **400BC** The area invaded by a Celtic tribe, the Boii, who give Bohemia its name.

4th–5th centuries AD Arrival of the Slavs.

7th century The first Bohemian state is established, ruled by a Frankish merchant named Samo.

9th–14th century Bohemia is ruled by princes from the Přemyslid dynasty. The first Prague Castle is built.

921–35 Prince Wenceslas (Václav) is killed by his brother Boleslav I. St Wenceslas later becomes patron saint of Bohemia.

973 Founding of the bishopric of Prague.

1085 Prince Vladislav is proclaimed first king of Bohemia by Emperor Henry IV.

1158 Prince Vladislav II becomes King Vladislav I. He founds Strahov Monastery and has the first stone bridge – the Judith Bridge – built across the Vltava.

1173–78 Prince Soběslav II. German migrants, arriving in ever-increasing numbers, are accorded equal rights.

1197–1230 King Přemsyl Otakar I. Emperor Frederick II confirms and extends the privileges of Bohemian kings. The throne becomes hereditary; under Wenceslas I (Václav I) the Old City is enlarged and fortified.

1253–78 Přemysl Otakar II. Bohemia becomes major power by conquering most of Austria. In 1257 the Lesser Quarter is granted a town charter. Otakar is killed in Battle of Marchfeld 1278.

1306 Murder of King Wenceslas II (Václav) ends male line of Přemyslids.

1310–46 King John of Luxembourg marries Přemyslid Princess Elizabeth. He founds the Luxembourg dynasty and begins the construction of the Cathedral. Prague becomes archbishopric in 1344.

1346–78 King Charles I (from 1355 Emperor Charles IV). Prague experiences a 'Golden Age' and becomes the largest city in Central Europe. Charles founds the university in 1348 and has the New Town laid out. The city's most important Gothic buildings are built or started. The Golden Bull (1356) confirms the rights and internal autonomy of Bohemia.

1378–1419 King Wenceslas IV. In 1393 he has the Vicar General, John of Nepomuk, thrown into the Vltava from the Charles Bridge. Jan Hus becomes rector of the university and preaches in Czech at the Bethlehem Chapel, so coming into conflict with Catholic establishment. In 1415 he is burnt at the stake in Constance.

1419–36 The Hussite Wars. On 30 July 1419, Hussites led by Jan Želivský throw members of King's Council from a window of the New Town Hall (First Defenestration of Prague). After the death of King Wenceslas, Czechs refuse the claim to the throne of his brother, Emperor Sigismund. At Battle of Vítkov, 14 July 1420, Hussites under Jan Žižka repel the emperor's armies; they then divide into two camps: moderate Utraquists, based in Prague, and radical Taborites, based in Tábor. In 1433 the Utraquists agree a compromise with the Catholics. In 1436 Sigismund is recognised as King of Bohemia, but dies the following year.

1458–71 King George of Poděbrady, leader of the Utraquists, later known as the 'Hussite King'. He is succeeded by Jagiellon kings of Poland: Vladislav II (1471–1516) and Louis (1516–26). After Louis's death at battle of Mohacs in southern Hungary, the throne of Bohemia and Hungary passes to the Habsburgs, who subsequently rule Bohemia until 1918.

1576–1612 Emperor Rudolf II. Prague becomes the imperial residence once more, experiencing a second 'Golden Age'. Famous artists and scientists from all over Europe work for king. With his 'Letter of Majesty' (1609) he grants the Bohemian estates freedom of religious worship. He is succeeded by his brother Matthias (1611–19).

1618–48 The Second Defenestration of Prague *(see page 31)* unleashes the Bohemian War, which develops into the Thirty Years' War. The leader of Protestant Union, Elector Frederick V of Palatinate, is appointed King of Bohemia (1619), but his forces are defeated on 8 November 1620 in Battle of the White Mountain by Catholics under Duke Maximilian of Bavaria. Frederick, the 'Winter King', flees to Netherlands. On 21 June 1621, Emperor Ferdinand II has 27 leaders of uprising executed in front of Old Town Hall. Some 150,000 Bohemian Protestants go into exile. The country becomes Catholic again, ruled by new aristocracy loyal to the emperor. In 1648, Swedish troops occupy Hradčany Castle and the Lesser Quarter, but fail to capture the Old Town. After their withdrawal, reconversion to Catholicism continues.

1680 Uprising of Bohemian peasants against the feudal system of government. Catholic and German dominance of spiritual life becomes all-embracing. Baroque art reaches its zenith.

1711–40 Emperor Charles VI. The Counter-Reformation gains greater influence; more people leave country.

1740–80 Maria Theresa. During War of Austrian Succession, the armies of Bavaria, Saxony and France capture Prague (1741). In 1744 Prussian troops besiege the city. In 1757, during the Seven Years' War, Prague is subjected to attack by Prussians, but the siege is lifted following Frederick the Great's defeat at Kolín. Maria Theresa has the damage repaired and Prague Castle extended.

1780–90 Emperor Joseph II. The last vestiges of Bohemian autonomy disappear. Serfdom is abolished in 1781, and the Jews are awarded civic rights. In 1784 the administrations of Hradčany, the Lesser Quarter, the Old Town and the New Town, as well as Jewish quarter, are amalgamated under a single magistrature.

1792–1835 Emperor Francis II (from 1804 Francis I of Austria). During the Napoleonic Wars the country is overrun on several occasions by French and Russian troops; freedom movements continue to be repressed. Rapid industrial expansion makes Bohemia and Moravia the most prosperous region in the Habsburg empire.

1835–48 Emperor Ferdinand I. Chancellor Metternich continues the repressive course in Bohemia, and there are growing tensions with Czechs demanding parity of their language with German and the establishment of movements against absolutism and centralism.

1848 Under the leadership of historian František Palacký, the Slavic Congress assembles in Prague. The Whit Uprising of the Czech working class, students and artisans is brutally crushed by Prince Windischgraetz and his Austrian forces.

1848–1916 Emperor Francis Joseph I. The Austro-Prussian War of 1866, fought mainly on Bohemian soil, ends in the Peace of Prague, whereby Austria and the Bohemian lands withdraw from the German Alliance. Universal suffrage is introduced in Bohemia in 1907. This period sees a renaissance of Czech cultural life in Prague, embodied in the construction of the National Theatre and National Museum, and the Czech composers Smetana, Dvořák and Janáček.

1914–18 World War I. The Estrangement between Czechs and Germans intensifies. In London, Paris and Washington, T.G. Masaryk, Eduard Beneš and others work towards the creation of Czechoslovakia.

1918 After the collapse of Austria-Hungary, the Republic of Czechoslovakia proclaimed in Prague. T.G. Masaryk is the first president.

1935 Resignation of Masaryk (d 1937) at age of 85; Edvard Beneš, previously Foreign Minister, becomes President.

1938 The Munich Agreement cedes the Sudetenland to Germany. Beneš is succeeded in office by Emil Hácha.

1939 President Hácha capitulates to Hitler in Berlin (15 March). The Reich Protectorate of Bohemia and Moravia is proclaimed, and German troops occupy the country.

1939–45 World War II. In 1942, German Reichsprotektor Reinhard Heydrich is assassinated in Prague. Those responsible are eventually hunted down and killed in the Church of St Carlo Borromeo, and the village of Lidice is exterminated. Of the Jewish community of almost 40,000 in Prague, 36,000 are murdered. On 5 May 1945 rebellion breaks out in Prague. Four days later the city is occupied by the Red Army. Beneš becomes President again. Some 3½ million Sudeten Germans are dispossessed and deported; more than 240,000 die.

1948 Czechoslovakia becomes a People's Republic. Klement Gottwald is president.

1960 A new constitution proclaims the transition to a Socialist Republic.

1968 Alexander Dubček becomes Secretary General of the Communist Party. The policy of 'Socialism with human face' encounters the disapproval of the Soviet Union and other Warsaw Pact members. The country is invaded on 21 August.

1969 Czechoslovakia becomes a Federal State on 1 January. On 17 April, Dubček is replaced by Gustáv Husák as party chief.

1977 Foundation of the civil rights group known as 'Charter 77'.

1989–90 Mass demonstrations and a general strike in November and December (Velvet Revolution) lead to the resignation of the government and the introduction of a multi-party system. The dramatist and leader of the Civic Forum, Václav Havel, becomes president. In April 1990 the country's name is changed to Czech and Slovak Federal Republic.

1992–3 On 17 July Slovakia declares independence and Havel resigns. On 1 January the Czech and Slovak Republics become independent states, and Havel re-elected President of the Czech Republic.

1994–8 Prague is politically turbulent following accusations of official corruption.

1999 The Czech Republic joins NATO.

2002 Severe flooding hits the city.

2003 President Václav Havel steps down. Václav Klaus is elected president.

2004 The Czech Republic joins the EU.

2005 Jiří Paroubek made prime minister.

Maps below & page 22

Preceding pages: the Old Town Square
Below: view of Hradčany

1: Prague Castle

Occupying a commanding position high above the River Vltava, ★★★ **Prague Castle** (Pražský hrad; Apr–Oct: daily 9am–5pm; Nov–Mar: daily 9am–4pm; www.hrad.cz) ❶ is the most extensive complex of buildings in the city. It forms part of the historic district of Hradčany, which stretches as far as the Strahov Monastery *(see page 47)*.

ACCESS

There are a number of different ways of getting to the Castle:

1. By Metro, the castle can be approached from the north. From Wenceslas Square, you should take the underground *(Line A)* as far as Malostranská station, where, by following the Staré zámecké schody (Old Castle Steps) uphill, you can reach the east end of the castle in about five minutes. Alternatively, if you get out at Hradčanská station, you can walk along Tychonova to the Belvedere *(see page 40)*, through the garden and thence to the North Gate of the castle. You can also take the tram for one stop to the Prašný most, and walk for about five minutes along the U prašného mostů, to reach the North Gate of the castle,

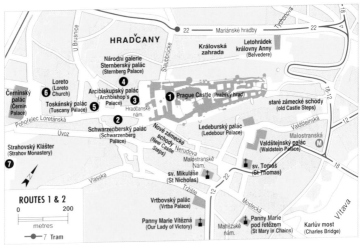

through which you should then pass into the Second Castle Courtyard *(see page 22)*. The North Gate can also be reached directly by tram No. 22 from the city centre, boarding in front of the Tesco department store in Spálená, or in front of the National Theatre. Alternatively, you can turn off to the right in front of the gate and pass through the Castle Garden *(see page 39)* and thence to the main courtyard, the point from which the route described on page 21 actually begins.

2. Visitors on foot can choose between two ascents which lead from the Lesser Quarter:

a) The climb from the Lesser Quarter Square (Malostranské náměstí) takes about 15 minutes and leads through Zámecká and via the Nové zámecké schody (New Castle Steps) to Hradčany Square (Hradčanské náměstí).

b) The Staré zámecké schody begins near the Malostranská underground station and emerges at the east end of the castle. This route is, however, more suitable for the return journey after viewing the castle.

Another approach is to turn from the Lesser Quarter Square (Malostranské náměstí) into Nerudova, then bearing right onto the castle approach ramp (Ke Hradu – closed to all motor vehicles), which leads up to Hradčany Square.

3. If you are travelling by car you should take the Malostranské náměstí and then Letenská, since Neruda is barred to motor traffic. Following Klárov, Chotkova, Mariánské hradby, Jelení and Keplerova, you will eventually come to Pohořelec Square (which can also be reached from the Old Town via the Cechuv Bridge or the Hlákuv Bridge). You should then continue on foot along Loretánská until you reach Hradčany Square (Hradčanské náměstí).

Star Attraction
● **Prague Castle**

Tickets
Information and tickets for the historic buildings of the castle are available from the Information Centre in the Third Courtyard (daily, Apr–Oct 9am–5pm, Nov–Mar 9am–4pm; tel: 224 373 368).

Steps to the Castle

HISTORY

The history of Prague Castle is closely linked with that of the city as summarised on pages 13–15.

Nothing remains today of the first wooden fortress, built on the bare hill near the ford across the Vltava during the second half of the

Maps on pages 18 & 22

Renaissance Man
The man who embodied the Renaissance in Prague was Emperor Rudolf II (1576–1611) – a voracious collector of artwork and curiosities from around the world, a great patron of artists, and a dabbler in alchemy and the occult. When he moved the Imperial Residence from Vienna to Prague in 1583, it sparked Bohemia's Renaissance and an economic boom.

Castle guard

9th century. In 1950, remains were discovered of the Church of St Mary, which was built at about the same time; they can be seen at the end of the Castle Gallery. In about 915–20, the Basilica of St George was built, which, however, had to be rebuilt after 1142 following a fire. In 926–9, Prince Wenceslas the Saintly erected a small Romanesque round church (rotunda) in honour of St Vitus; it stood on the site which is now occupied by the Wenceslas Chapel of St Vitus' Cathedral.

During the 11th and 12th centuries, the old wooden castle was replaced by a Romanesque building, which today forms the lowest storey of the former Royal Palace *(see page 29)*. In 1061–91, a Romanesque basilica was erected in place of the St Vitus Rotunda mentioned above. The remains of this construction can be seen behind the statue of St George.

GOTHIC AND RENAISSANCE

During the 13th and 14th centuries, in the reigns of Otakar II, Charles IV and Wenceslas IV, the present middle storey of the former Royal Palace was built. Work started on the construction of St Vitus' Cathedral in 1344. Until 1352 the project was supervised by Matthew of Arras, then until 1399 by Peter Parler and finally by the latter's sons. By this time the choir had been completed, as had the Wenceslas Chapel, the eastern section of the nave, the south porch and parts of the south tower.

During the Late Gothic era, the former Royal Palace acquired its present upper floor under Vladislav II (1471–1516), including the Vladislav Hall, the castle walls and fortified towers.

When the Habsburg emperor Ferdinand I ascended the throne of Bohemia in 1526, the purely Gothic appearance of the castle underwent rapid and radical changes. Spacious parks and gardens were laid out, and new audience halls and offices as well as the Belvedere pleasure palace were added. Under Emperor Rudolf II, Prague Castle enjoyed its cultural heyday, becoming the focal point of the empire once again, as it had been during the reign of Charles IV.

MARIA THERESA'S MODERNISATION

It was not until the 18th century, however, that Castle Hill finally lost its medieval appearance. The Empress Maria Theresa ordered the repair and modernisation of the buildings, which had been badly damaged during the Seven Years' War. By filling in the moat on the west side, redesigning the first castle courtyard, and erecting a number of buildings linking together existing wings, Hradčany Castle was given its present – late baroque and neoclassical – appearance.

Only St Vitus' Cathedral, which from 1419 had been left untouched apart from a single four-year building phase, had to wait many more years for its completion: work started in 1872 and was not finished until 1929.

Below: the Second Courtyard
Bottom: Changing of the Guard parade

TOUR OF PRAGUE CASTLE

As is evident from the various routes listed on pages 18–19, one way of viewing Prague Castle is from west (Hradčany Square) to east (Staré zámecké schody/Old Castle Steps). The main sights to be visited will then be the Castle Gallery, the Chapel of the Holy Cross with the Cathedral Treasure, St Vitus' Cathedral, the former Royal Palace, St George's Church and the Golden Lane. You can also start the tour from the opposite end, beginning at the Staré zámecké schody.

Maps
on pages
22, 23, 25

Maps on pages 22, 23, 25

Founding Father
The bronze statue facing the entrance to the First Courtyard is Thomas Garrigue Masaryk, the first president of the first Czechoslovak Republic, which existed between the wars. Masaryk – the first democratic leader to sit in the Castle – was an unflinchingly moral man and a sometimes controversial professor at Charles University. In a sense, he paved the way for Václav Havel, the country's next philosopher-president.

If you arrive by bus, the most convenient tour is one beginning and ending at Hradčany Square. It leads from the Entrance Courtyard to the Second Courtyard with the Chapel of the Holy Cross, the Third Courtyard with St Vitus' Cathedral and the former Royal Palace, St George's Church, the Golden Lane and back via the Mihulka Tower to the Second Courtyard with the Castle Gallery, the former Riding School and the Spanish Hall.

A SERIES OF COURTYARDS

From Hradčany Square you first enter the **Entrance Courtyard**, also known as the First Courtyard. It was designed by the Viennese architect Nikolaus von Pacassi, who, on instructions from Maria Theresa, had the moat on the west side of the castle filled in and some old buildings demolished and new ones erected. The fighting giants at the entrance (replicas since 1912) were sculpted by Ignaz Platzer the Elder between 1766–8. The Changing of the Guard takes place every hour on the hour.

Integrated into the new buildings, the **Matthias Gate**, dating from 1614, is the oldest secular baroque edifice in Prague; it was the work of Vincenzo Scamozzi, the architect of the New Law Courts in Venice. From the gateway, a staircase on the right leads up to the reception rooms of the President of the Czech Republic.

Behind the gateway is the **Second Courtyard**. This was also completely redesigned by Pacassi during the 18th century. Straight ahead you will see the former **Chapel of the Holy Cross** (Kaple sv. Kříž), built by Anselmo Lurago in 1753. The treasure of St Vitus' Cathedral, previously on display here, is no longer on view.

On the left (north) side wall of the Second Courtyard is the entrance to the Castle Gallery *(see page 38)*.

On the way into the Third Courtyard, you will pass the lovely baroque fountain,

Belvedere
Daliborka
Tower
Old Castle
Steps
Singing ★
Fountain
Black
★ Tower
Toy Museum ★
Lobkowitz
Palace
The Golden
Lane
White
Tower
Former Convent
of Noble Women
Basilica of
St George
Former Royal Gardens
Old ★
Bohemian
Art
St
George's ★
Square
Story of
Prague Castle
South
Gardens
Ball
House
Former
Royal Palace
Mihulka
Tower
St Vitus'
Cathedral
Third
Courtyard
Old Chapter
House
Monolith
Paradise
Gardens
Former
Riding
School
Prašný
most
Chapel of
the Holy
Cross
New Castle
Steps
Castle
Gallery
Second
Courtyard
First
Courtyard
Matthias
Gate
Castle
Gardens
Hradčany
Square
Moat
Deer
Moat

**PRAGUE CASTLE
(PRAŽSKÝ HRAD)**

created by Hieronymus Kohl in 1686. There is a post office in the building between the two courtyards; its entrance is in the Third Courtyard.

ST VITUS' CATHEDRAL

Opposite the connecting passage to the **Third Courtyard**, the (Neo-Gothic) silhouette of St Vitus' Cathedral soars heavenwards. Together with the new buildings on the south side, erected by Pacassi during the 18th century, the cathedral dominates the appearance of the courtyard. If you have sufficient time, it is worth walking once round the cathedral before entering via the main door, in order to gain a first overall impression of this magnificent example of sacred architecture.

★★★ **St Vitus' Cathedral** (Svatý Víta) was built over the remains of a Romanesque rotunda (926–9) and a Romanesque basilica (1061–96). Construction work was interrupted in 1419 by the Hussite Wars and was not completed until more than 500 years later (in 1929 under the direction of the Slovenian architect Josip Plečnik), using the original plans as far as possible and skilfully adding modern building elements. In the sketch at the bottom of this page you will also find marked the positions of the Romanesque rotunda of St Vitus', the Roman-esque basilica, the Gothic section and the Neo-Gothic additions.

PORTALS AND WINDOWS

On the west front of the cathedral is the **main entrance**, with three bronze portals dating from 1927–9. The history of the building of the cathedral from 929–1929 is depicted in the middle; to the left is the legend of St Wenceslas, and to the right that of St Adalbert. The enormous rose window, which has a diameter of 10.4m (34ft), portrays the Creation and is made up of 26,740 separate panes of glass. The interior is 124m (407ft) long, 60m (197ft) wide and 34m (111ft) high; the most notable features are the 21 chapels, which contain a large number of important works of art.

Star Attraction

● **St Vitus' Cathedral**

St Vitus' Cathedral showing the South Portal

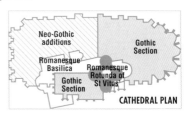

CATHEDRAL PLAN

Neo-Gothic additions

Romanesque Basilica

Gothic Section

Gothic Section

Romanesque Rotunda of St Vitus'

Map on page 25

The tour *(see plan on page 25)* begins on the left-hand side of the nave. In a side chapel on the left are ★ **stained glass windows** designed by the Prague art nouveau artist Alphonse Mucha *(see page 105)*, and featuring Saints Cyril and Methodius. The **organ loft** was built in 1559 by Bonifaz Wohlmuth. He was also responsible for the characteristic roof which caps the South Tower.

Below: Wenceslas Chapel
Bottom: the nave and choir

In the large **marble sarcophagus** in front of the high altar and directly above the Royal Crypt, Ferdinand I (died 1564), his beloved wife Anne of Bohemia and Hungary, and his son Maximilian II, lie buried. The Renaissance grating dates from 1589. Also of note are the Tomb of Count Schlick, designed in 1723 by Franz M Kaňka and executed by MB Braun; the gilt figures of the Bohemian patron saint *(c. 1700)* on the crossing; the pulpit (1631) and the contemporary windows (1946–7) at the end of the choir.

A SERIES OF CHAPELS

From here you enter the original Gothic section of the cathedral, designed by Peter Parler (show your ticket to the guard at the entrance to the ambulatory).

First comes the medieval **Chapel of St Sigismund**, with a baroque altar (1720) and tombs. The **Old Sacristy** follows with a painted statue

of St Michael (17th century), the painting *The Baptism of Christ* (1722) by Peter Brandl and the net vaulting designed by Peter Parler himself. Next are the **Chapel of St Anne**, with a silver reliquary plate (1266) and a Late Gothic portrait of the Virgin Mary, and the **Archbishops' Chapel** with a Renaissance tomb dating from 1582.

The three central choir chapels which now follow house the splendid Gothic tombs of six Bohemian princes and kings of the Přemyslid dynasty. They were commissioned by Emperor Charles IV and executed in 1376–7 by Peter Parler and his pupils.

Chapel of St John the Baptist contains: on the right, Břetislav II (1092–1100); on the left, Bořivoj II (1101–7).

Chapel of the Virgin Mary: on the right, Břetislav I (1034–55); on the left, Spytihnšv II (1055–61); Relief of Calvary (1621).

The **Chapel of Relics**: to the right, Přemsyl Otakar I (1197–1230), by Peter Parler himself; to the left, Přemsyl Otakar II (1253–78); you can also see the remains of Gothic frescoes.

> **Principal architects**
> In the Wallenstein or Mary Magdalene Chapel are the tombstones of the architects Matthew of Arras and Peter Parler, two of the principal builders of the cathedral. Matthew of Arras laid the initial groundwork as early as 1344, but after the architect's death, Emperor Charles IV chose 23-year-old Parler to complete his vision. Parler added his own distinctive genius to the cathedral, including the interior's unprecedented net vaulting.

VLADISLAV ORATORY

In the **Chapel of St John Nepomuk** you can see the remains of Gothic frescoes, a Late Gothic statue of the Virgin (*c.* 1500) and four silver busts of saints dating from about 1700. Opposite the chapel stands the magnificent ★**Memorial to St John Nepomuk**, designed by Josef Emanuel Fischer von Erlach and executed by the Viennese silversmith Johann Joseph Würth. The design of the figurative decoration was the work of several artists.

Continuing along the ambulatory is the **Vladislav Oratory**, built in 1493 as a gallery and connected by a cloister with the former Royal Palace. Also worth studying is the Late Gothic ribbed vaulting. This is followed by the Chapel of the Holy Cross and the **Martinitz Chapel**. Close by can be seen two large wooden

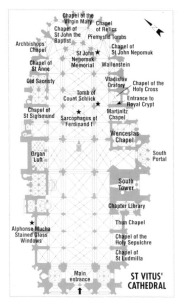

ST VITUS' CATHEDRAL

Maps
on pages
22 & 25

Interesting reliefs
Opposite the Chapel of St Anne are two large-scale wooden reliefs by Georg Bendl, representing the flight of the 'Winter King' Frederick of the Palatinate after the Battle of the White Mountain (1620). Of particular interest is the portrayal of the city at that time.

St John Nepomuk Memorial

reliefs carved by Georg Bendl in 1630, representing the devastation of the cathedral by the Calvinist iconoclasts in 1619.

ROYAL CRYPT

From the **Chapel of the Holy Cross**, steps lead down to the Romanesque rooms underneath the cathedral and the ★ **Royal Crypt**, which was redesigned in 1928–35. At the end of the passage a window looks into the chamber containing the royal tombs. Within nine sarcophagi lie Charles IV (centre), Ladislas Postumus (right), George of Poděbrady (left), Wenceslas IV and (facing in the opposite direction) his brother Johann von Görlitz, Rudolf II and Charles IV's four wives. At the end of the crypt, in an Empire-style coffin, lies Archduchess Maria Amalie, the daughter of Empress Maria Theresa, and – in a shared coffin – members of the family of Charles IV.

WENCESLAS CHAPEL

Next you will come to the loveliest and most precious section of the cathedral, the ★★ **Wenceslas Chapel** (Kapel sv. Václav). This chapel was erected in 1362–7 by Peter Parler above the remains of the Romanesque rotunda. It has been meticulously restored in recent years, and houses the tomb of the patron saint of Bohemia, St Wenceslas, as well as relics and a statue (1373).

The walls are decorated with a patchwork of polished gemstones (jasper, amethysts, agate, carnelian, emeralds), as well as fine gilding and frescoes. The lower row of frescoes (14th century) depicts the Passion of Christ, while those above (*c.* 1509) portray the legend of St Wenceslas. The bronze ring at the entrance to the chapel is thought to be the very one to which St Wenceslas clung as he was murdered by his brother Boleslav.

Above the chapel, in the Crown Chapel (not open to the public), which has a door with seven locks, the Bohemian coronation insignia have been kept since 1625.

Neo-Gothic Chapels

On the left is the entrance to the **South Tower** (96m/315ft), with a fine view of Hradčany and the city (the tower is closed in winter). This is followed by the **Chapter Library** which houses a collection of old manuscripts. The tour finishes with a series of Neo-Gothic chapels: the **Thun Chapel**, with modern windows and a number of old tombs; the **Chapel of the Holy Sepulchre**; and the **Chapel of St Ludmilla**.

The **view** down the nave from in front of the main doors is spectacular. From here the genius of Peter Parler is evident, particularly compared to the rather wooden Neo-Gothic additions.

Star Attraction
● Wenceslas Chapel

Equestrian Statue

Passing once more through the Main Entrance, you should return to the Third Castle Courtyard, and then skirt round the cathedral to the left. You will pass the Old Presbytery (17th century), the Monolith in Mrakotin granite erected in 1928 in memory of the victims of World War I, and a replica of the **equestrian statue of St George**. The original (1373), by the brothers Márton and György Kolozsvári, is considered one of the most important examples of Gothic statuary. Here you will also see the remains of the Romanesque basilica (11th century).

Below: equestrian statue of St George
Bottom: stained glass windows by Alphonse Mucha

Maps
on pages
22, 25, 29

SOUTH TOWER

You will then arrive at the ★ **South Tower** *(see also page 27)*, the work of Peter Parler, his sons Johann and Wenceslas (14th century), Hans Tirol and Bonifaz Wohlmuth (16th century) and Nicolò Pacassi (18th century). Together with the South Portal and the outside wall of the Wenceslas Chapel *(see page 26)*, the tower makes up the most attractive and impressive section of the cathedral: the South Front. It was completed not in Gothic but in Renaissance style; during the 19th century, the main entrance was transferred from the south to the west side of the building.

SOUTH PORTAL

Designed by Peter Parler, the ★ **South Portal** of the cathedral, also known as the 'Golden Portal', is a triple-arched arcade, narrowing at the back towards a slender door to allow for the abutting Wenceslas Chapel.

Nowhere else are the extraordinary skills of the architect so evident as here, in the delicate ribs that support the three Gothic arches. This was the main cathedral entrance right up until the 19th century, and it is still used today on special occasions. The modern, attractive bronze grating, with representations of the months of the year, was completed in 1954 by sculptor Jaroslav Horejec.

> **Glass mosaic**
> Of particular note on the South Portal is the glass mosaic above the door, produced in 1370–1 by Venetian artists, and the first of its kind north of the Alps. It portrays the Last Judgment. Apart from glass, small pieces of quartz and other natural stones were employed; the golden effect was achieved by laying thick sheets of gold foil between two stones. As well as depicting the Biblical scenes of the Resurrection of the Dead and the Last Judgment, the picture also portrays the Virgin Mary, St John the Baptist, the apostles, Charles IV and his wife Elizabeth of Pomerania, as well as the six patron saints of Bohemia.

Last Judgement mosaic

THE ROYAL PALACE

The right-hand (south) section of the Third Castle Courtyard includes a wing which – like the Entrance Courtyard and the Second Courtyard *(see page 22)* – was designed during the reign of Maria Theresa by Pacassi. The large portico with the balcony (designed by Ignaz Platzer, 1760–1) today forms the entrance to the Presidential Chancellery. The former **Royal Palace** (Starý královský palác) is linked to the Pacassi buildings; today, the palace includes a Romanesque, an Early Gothic and a Late Gothic storey.

The tour begins on the upper storey (Late Gothic). To the side of the palace, a ramp leads down into the former palace courtyard to the Early Gothic central storey. To the right, under the portico designed by Pacassi, is the main entrance. From the **antechamber** turn left, initially into the **Green Room**, where, on 23 May 1618, the Bohemian estates assembled shortly before the Second Defenestration of Prague *(see page 31)*. Continue into the **Vladislav Room**, vaulted in 1490–3, adorned with the monogram of Vladislav and the coats of arms of Bohemia, Moravia, Luxembourg, Silesia and Poland.

VLADISLAV AUDIENCE HALL

Returning to the antechamber, the next room on the left is the famous ★★**Vladislav Audience Hall** (Vladislavský sál), regarded as the finest Late Gothic room in Central Europe. It was built between 1493 and 1502 by Benedikt Ried as a Throne Room and also served as a jousting hall; it is 62m (203ft) long, 16m (52ft) wide and up to 13m (43ft) high. In view of the two storeys that lie below the hall, the construction of the vast space without supporting pillars was a remarkable architectural feat for its time.

Of particular note are the artistically interwoven ribs forming the vaulting. Today the national president is elected in the former Throne Room.

Star Attraction
● Vladislav Audience Hall

Vladislav Audience Hall

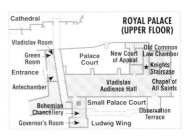

ROYAL PALACE
(UPPER FLOOR)

Cathedral
Vladislav Room
Green Room
Entrance
Antechamber
Palace Court
New Court of Appeal
Old Common Law Chamber
★ Knights Staircase
Vladislav Audience Hall
Chapel of All Saints
Bohemian Chancellery
Small Palace Court
Governor's Room
Ludwig Wing
Observation Terrace

Maps
on pages
23, 25, 29

Scene of Defenestration

On the right-hand-side of the Vladislav Audience Hall is the entrance into the so-called Ludwig Wing, which was extended in 1503–10 by Benedict Ried and contains the offices of the **Bohemian Chancellery**. The first room is the Chamber of Scribes and Secretaries, with the coat of arms of King Ludwig (1516–26) and a model of the castle during the 18th century which clearly shows the cathedral in its unfinished state.

In the **Governor's Room** next door, on 23 May 1618, the imperial governors Jaroslav Martinic and Vilém Slavata, and their private secretary Philipp Fabricius, were thrown from the east (left-hand) window 16m (52ft) into the castle moat below. The victims survived by landing in a dung heap (a fact attributed by Catholics to the intevention of angels), but the deed precipitated the Thirty Years' War *(see panel on facing page)*.

On the way back to the Vladislav Hall, you can ascend via the linking passageway to the Imperial Court Chancellery if it is open, and then across into the Vladislav Oratory in St Vitus' Cathedral.

Chapel of All Saints

Chapel of All Saints

In the Vladislav Hall, cross to the opposite (east) side wall. Under a three-section Renaissance window (*c.* 1500) and through a doorway added in 1598, there is a balcony above the **Chapel of All Saints**. A Gothic chapel was added here on the site of a Romanesque royal chapel, subsequently completed by Peter Parler. The chapel was later destroyed during the great castle fire of 1541, then rebuilt in Renaissance style in 1570–1. During the rebuild it was extended as far as the Vladislav Hall and linked to it by means of this doorway.

Within the chapel, of note are the *Descent from the Cross* by Hans von Aachen (1552–1615), as well as a 12-painting picture cycle in the choir dating from 1699, by Christian Dittmann. It shows scenes from the life of St Prokop, who was buried here. On the High Altar is the painting entitled *All Saints* by Wenceslas Lorenz Reinder (1689–1743).

OBSERVATION TERRACE

Return once more to the Vladislav Hall and turn left to emerge onto the **Observation Terrace** (closed in winter). This gives a fine view of the town and (to the left) the outside façade of the Chapel of All Saints and the Noblewomen's Convent as well as (to the right) the exterior façade of the Vladislav Hall and the adjoining Ludwig Wing with the offices of the Bohemian Chancellery *(see opposite)*. The very last window is the one from which the Second Defenestration of Prague took place in 1618.

OLD COMMON LAW CHAMBER

Crossing the Vladislav Hall again, you will then enter the ★ **Old Common Law Chamber**. Dating from the reign of Wenceslas IV, the room was rebuilt by Benedikt Ried in about 1500 and restored in 1559–63 by Bonifaz Wohlmuth, following the Great Fire of 1541. The stone Renaissance gallery for the senior clerk is by Wohlmuth; the furnishings – based on old models – date from the 19th century. The royal throne is on the window side; the archbishop's throne and the benches for the clergy are on the left, whilst the seats of the estates officials and lords temporal are on the right. On the walls are copies of paintings of Habsburg rulers (18th and 19th centuries).

> **Second Defenestration**
> When Ferdinand II began to renege on Rudolf II's 'Letter of Majesty' (guaranteeing religious freedom and the unrestricted building of churches), by harshly repressing the Protestant population, an enraged populace threw two governors of Bohemia and their personal secretary out of the Council Room window at the castle on 23 May 1618. This event, which has become known as the 'Second Defenestration of Prague', unleashed the Thirty Years' War between Catholics and Protestants.

Old Common Law Chamber

Map on page 29

The sessions of the Bohemian estates were held in this chamber until 1847. Today, the national president formally signs the election protocol here following his election.

ROYAL ARCHIVES

Nearby, the **Knights' Staircase** leads down to the middle storey *(see opposite)*. Ignore this for now and ascend the spiral staircase to the chancelleries of the Estates Chronicles and the Royal Archives. The Estates Chronicles were books in which important resolutions, the ownership status of towns and monasteries, and the property owned by important individuals were recorded from the 13th century onwards.

In the small **Estates Chancellery Room** are tables dating from the 17th century; on the walls are painted the coats of arms of the leading officials. The Estates Chronicles were kept in the baroque cupboards of the Estates Chancellery Chamber, and in a carved wooden cupboard dating from 1562 in the adjacent main Estates Chancellery Room. The Royal Archive was converted into a meeting chamber for the estates authorities in 1737; from 1838–1884 the room housed the Royal Archives, a collection of privileges belonging to the Bohemian crown. Nowadays, the Estates Chancellery houses a permanent exhibition illustrating the duties of that body.

Hitler's crown

The room housing the Parler sculptures in the former Royal Palace was used to store the crown jewels during World War II. While it's never been confirmed, locals tell the tale of how Adolf Hitler marched into this room and donned the crown out of hubris after he entered Prague in 1938. Little did the Führer know, an old legend says that anyone who dares to wear the crown jewels and is not the kingdom's rightful ruler will not remain long on this earth.

Players in the palace

KNIGHTS' STAIRCASE

Returning once again to the Vladislav Hall, you should bear left towards the ★ **Knights' Staircase**, passing en route the New Court of Appeal (left). The staircase was constructed by Benedikt Ried in 1500 and has a magnificent rib vaulted ceiling. It enabled the knights who were to take part in indoor jousting competions to ride on horseback from the palace courtyard into the Vladislav Hall.

You should leave the upper storey of the former Royal Palace via the Knights' Staircase, which will bring you to the entrance to the Romanesque lower storey. Descending a steep staircase, you will come to the former South Gate of the Romanesque palace.

After passing the remnants of the palace fortifications, dating from the 9th century, you will enter a room built in about 1140. It is 33m (108ft) long, and leads into another, more recent room housing copies of the sculptures by Peter Parler in St Vitus' Cathedral.

OLD ESTATES CHANCELLERY CHAMBER

One of the last rooms on the tour of the exhibition, and one of the most impressive, is the ★ **Old Estates Chancellery Chamber**, which has a vaulted ceiling supported by two squat pillars. It was built during the 13th century under Přemysl Otakar II and served as the repository for the Estates records, the books in which the properties of the higher estates and the most important resolutions of the Estates Council were recorded.

Two additional interesting rooms which originally formed part of the exhibition are in the so-called Charles Palace. They both date from the 14th century, but are at present closed to the public.

THE STORY OF PRAGUE CASTLE

This newly opened exhibition – beautifully displayed – can be reached by the ramp to the left of the entrance to the Old Royal Palace. This highly recommended introduction to the castle

Below: coats of arms in the Estates Chancellery Room
Bottom: Knights' Staircase

Maps on pages 22 & 29

Below: Basilica of St George, viewed from St Vitus'
Bottom: façade detail with St George slaying the dragon

site (*see* www.story-castle.cz) has two parts: the first leads you from room to room describing the development of the castle in chronological order; the second tells the "Story of …" various subjects, such as residences, learning, burials, the Church and patronage. The exhibits are well-labelled in English and Czech, and there is a "Castle Game" for children to play that takes them around the displays gathering information, role-playing, and writing and drawing.

The story of the castle site is told from prehistory to the 20th century. Among the exhibits that illustrate the history of the castle are: a helmet and chainmail coat said to have belonged to St Václav; the tympanum of the Bazilika sv. Jiří *(see below)*; the grave dresses of Rudolf II and Eleonora of Toledo; and some amazing examples of 16th- and 17th-century costume.

BASILICA OF ST GEORGE

After visiting the former Royal Palace, the tour of the castle continues across Castle Hill. Under the passageway, linking the palace with the Vladislav Oratory in the Cathedral, stands the unadorned west façade of the ★★**Basilica of St George** (Bazilika svátého Jiří). The true character of this, the most important Romanesque

building in the city, does not become evident until you step inside. Built in 915–20, the church was reconstructed following a fire in 1142. Between 1959 and 1962 it was completely restored and many later additions were removed.

The triple-naved basilica is regarded as the oldest example of Romanesque architecture in Prague. Today, apart from its attraction as a historic monument, the building also serves as a concert hall.

Worthy of note are the 14th-century tombs of two Dukes of Bohemia: Vratislav I (*c*. 920) on the left and Boleslav II (967–99) on the right. Behind lies the crypt, with six slender columns, and one of the most important pieces of Romanesque sculpture in Bohemia: a triple relief created in about 1230 portraying the Virgin Mary with Mlada and Berta – the first abbesses of the Convent of St George – and King Otakar I and his sister Agnes.

Also of interest are the raised east choir with an 18th-century double staircase and the remains of Romanesque frescoes (up on the right near the choir), the Chapel of St Ludmilla (14th century) with the Saints' Crypt and St Mary's Chapel (below, to the left of the choir).

BAROQUE AND MANNERIST ART

To the north of the Basilica of St George stand the former monastery buildings, which house the **★★ Collection of Baroque and Mannerist Art** (Tues–Sun 10am–6pm, www.ngprague.cz). On the ground floor can be seen the original carved lintel from the side entrance of the Basilica of St George. The collection proper is on the upper floor. One of the most extraordinary exhibits is a Tree of Life (*c*. 1650) from southern Germany carved from a wide variety of woods. Notable among the works on display by Bohemian painters are the *Bust of the Talking Apostle* painted in 1725 by Petr Brandl (1668–1735), and the *Self Portrait* (1711) by Jan Kupecký (1667–1740), which shows the artist working on a portrait of his wife. There are also two delightful landscapes by Roland Savery (1576–1639).

Star Attractions
● **Basilica of St George**
● **Collection of Baroque and Mannerist Art**

St George's altarpiece

Map
on page
22

Emperor of Alchemy

Contrary to popular legend, the goldsmiths and alchemists employed by Rudolf II never lived on Golden Lane. But the eccentric ruler, who reigned from 1583–1611, was deeply interested in both riches and magic. Rather than housing his court alchemists in the Castle on Golden Lane, he used a network of ancient tunnels extending beneath the Lesser Quarter and Old Town to give his occult advisers access to Hradčany.

THE GOLDEN LANE

Continuing along Jiřská, you should notice on the south façade of the basilica the Renaissance portal, created in 1510–20 by the school of Benedikt Ried. On the right is the former Convent of Noblewomen, built in 1754–5 to a design by Pacassi. A little further on there are steps leading down to Zlatá – ★ **The Golden Lane**, also known as the Goldmakers' or Alchemists' Lane.

The 18 tiny, colourfully painted houses were built into the arches of the northern wall to provide housing for minor craftsmen, including goldsmiths. In 1597 they were allocated to the 24 castle guards. Renovated in 1952–4, the houses form a sort of open-air museum. However, the houses are now shops, making the alley an over-popular tourist trap. Franz Kafka *(see page 106)* lived for a short while at No. 22, which now contains a tiny exhibition and bookshop.

BATTLEMENT WALK

Above the houses runs a battlement walk. Originally the walk linked the **White Tower** (Bílá věž), which served during the 16th and 17th centuries as state prison, and during the 18th century as a debtors' tower for noblemen, with the **Daliborka** (Dalibor Tower), a remnant of the Late Gothic castle defences.

The Golden Lane

In 1498 Knight Dalibor, the hero of Bedřich Smetana's opera of the same name *(see page 109)*, was held prisoner in the tower, which had been built in 1496 by Benedikt Ried. The only access to his actual cell is a small round opening which can still be seen today. There is a staircase leading down to the Black Tower at the upper end of the Staré zámecké schody (Old Castle Steps).

HISTORY MUSEUM

From The Golden Lane return to Jiřská, where you turn to the left. On your right you will see the former ★ **Lobkovický Palác** (Lobkowitz Palace), currently the **Národní Muzeum** of the history of Bohemia up to the revolution of 1848 (Tues–Sun 9am–5pm). The building also houses temporary exhibitions and is occasionally used as a concert hall. The palace was built during the second half of the 16th century in Italian Renaissance style. The items on display include the decree from Rudolf II ensuring religious freedom in Bohemia, and a room describing the events of 1848 revolution.

On the left is the former Office of the Senior Burgrave, which was built at about the same time. (The Senior Burgrave was the highest official in Bohemia, whose duty it was to represent the king during the latter's absence.) Today, the building is the **Toy Museum**, which has a large selection of toys from ancient Greece to the present day (daily 9.30am–5.30pm).

View from the ramparts

BLACK TOWER

At the end of Jiřská stands the **Black Tower** (Černá věž), whose origins reach back to the 12th century. On the far side, the Staré zámecké schody leads on down towards the River Vltava. If you wish to visit the remaining sights on Castle Hill, you should return to the square in front of St George's Church after viewing the Black Tower on Jiřská. Then you should turn right into Vikářská, which leads round the northern façade of St Vitus' Cathedral.

No. 37, called the Mladotův dům, is the location of the former Kapitel Library (no access to the public). The building has a ceiling decorated with notable frescoes dating from 1725; they are the work of the artist Jan Vodňanský.

The Black Tower

MIHULKA TOWER

Next door, at No. 38, is the entrance to the **Mihulka Tower**. Dating from the 13th century, this tower, the diameter of which is 20m (66ft), formed part of the the northern fortifications of Prague Castle and was used at various periods to store gunpowder. It houses a permanent exhibition consisting of an alchemist's workshop from the time of Emperor Rudolf II, as well as a number of portraits.

CASTLE GALLERY

Continuing along Vikářská, you will eventually come back to the Second Courtyard. On the right, you will find the entrance to the ★★ **Castle Gallery** (daily 10am–6pm). Since 1964, the former stables have housed the remains of the valuable Renaissance and baroque art collections assembled by the Habsburgs during the 16th and 17th centuries in Prague Castle. Much of the collection was looted by the Swedes when they occupied the city in 1648, nonetheless a number of excellent paintings remain. The collection was rehung in 1998, and the gallery is well worth a visit.

The room on the left holds works of the Gothic and early Renaissance. Notable works to be found here include the *Madonna with Sleeping Child* by Joos van Cleve (1465–1540), part of an altarpiece by Lucas Cranach the elder (1472–1553), and the *Portrait of Lady Vaux* by Hans Holbein the younger (1497–1543). Later works, on display in the remaining galleries, include paintings by Titian (1480–1576; *A Young Woman at Her Toilet*), Rubens (1577–1640; *Assembly of the Gods at Olympus*), Veronese (1528–88; *Portrait of Jakob König*) and Tintoretto (1519–94; *The Flagellation of Christ*).

THE GARDENS

At the end of the tour of Castle Hill proper, it is recommended you visit the park on the south slope, with its Paradise Garden and South Garden, as well as the Royal Garden to the northeast (daily, Apr–Oct 10am–6pm). In the Third Courtyard you will find the descent to the **Paradise Garden**. This charming park originally dates from 1562, but was redesigned in 1920–3 in accordance with plans drawn up by Josip Plečnik.

The circular structure adorning the gardens dates from 1614 when it was built for Emperor Matthias. The attractive weather vane on the roof displays the monogram of the ruler and his wife Anna. Inside the building it is still possible to see the original ceiling paintings, showing the emblems of all the countries in the Habsburg Empire. The wall paintings were completed much later, in 1848. The statue of the *Good Shepherd* in the garden was created by I. Kalvodas in 1922. A focal point of the park is provided by the huge granite basin weighing 40 tonnes.

SOUTH GARDEN

Immediately adjoining the Paradise Garden is the **South Garden** (Zahrada na valech). The park was laid out in 1928 (also designed by Josip Plečnik)

Star Attraction
● The Castle Gallery

Gardens to enjoy
The Paradise and South-gardens are very popular with the citizens of Prague as a destination for strolling. There are magnificent views of the city, and the parks offer an excellent impression of the south façade of the castle, below which they are situated.

South Garden and the Royal Palace

Map on page 22

'Singing' fountain
In front of the Belvedere in the Royal Gardens you'll find the (previously) Singing Fountain, designed by the Italian sculptor Francesco Terzio. Decorated with flowers, animals, Greek gods and even a bagpipe player, the fountain was a favourite among children for the sounds created by the hollow metal design. However, the fountain has been completely reconstructed and, unfortuantely, no longer sings.

on the site of the castle fortifications, which had been filled in towards the end of the 19th century.

Two baroque obelisks beneath the Ludwig Wing mark the spot where the two imperial governors, Martinicz and Slavata and their secretary *(see page 30)* were thrown from the castle window to the ground in 1618. This incident, known as the Second Defenestration of Prague, sparked off the Thirty Years' War.

THE ROYAL GARDEN

To the northeast of the castle, separated from the latter by the Deer Moat, lies the ★ **Royal Garden** (Královská zahrada), reached by taking the passage that leads from the Second Courtyard through to the North Gate and crossing the Prašný most bridge. On the left is the former **Riding School** (Jízdárna), built in about 1694, and between 1947 and 1950 converted into a gallery for exhibitions.

The Royal Garden is on the right. Laid out by Ferdinand I in 1534 and redesigned in 1955, it is a beautiful place for a stroll, particularly in spring when the tulips are in bloom. It also contains some fine garden architecture, including the **Ball House** (Míčnova), designed by Bonifaz Wohlmuth in 1563–8. Originally it was used for playing a form of real tennis, and is covered in exquisite *sgraffito* work.

The Belvedere

THE BELVEDERE

Continuing on through the garden, at the northeastern end you will arrive at what is considered to be the most important Renaissance building on Bohemian soil, the Royal Summer Palace, or ★ **Belvedere**, of Queen Anne (Letohrádek královny Anny), wife of Ferdinand I, the first Habsburg emperor (1526–64). The palace was built between 1538–63 and is the work of several architects, including (from 1538) Giovanni Spatio and (from 1557) Bonifaz Wohlmuth. The copper roof, whose shape recalls an upturned boat, was completed in 1560. The ground plan of the palace is modelled on that of the Temple of Poseidon at Paestum.

2: To Strahov Monastery

Prague Castle – Schwarzenberg Palace – Archbishop's Palace – National Gallery – Tuscany Palace – Loreto Church – Strahov Monastery

Map on page 18

This route covers three of the city's most important sights: the National Gallery, the Loreto Church and the former Strahov Monastery.

On Hradčany Square (Hradčanské náměstí), in front of **Prague Castle** (Pražsky hrad) ❶, stand three large palaces: the Schwarzenberg Palace to the south, the Tuscany Palace to the west and the Archbishop's Palace to the north.

Below: diamond monstrance at the Loreto Church
Bottom: Hradčany Square with the Archbishop's Palace

SCHWARZENBERG PALACE

The **Schwarzenberg Palace** ❷ was originally built in 1543 by Augustin Vlach for the Lobkowitz family, and was acquired by the Schwarzenberg family in 1714. It is one of the loveliest Renaissance buildings in Bohemia; of particular interest are the *sgraffito* paintings on the façades, the rectangular stones which – in the style of Italian models – have been worked to look like diamonds, as well as the main courtyard and the ceiling frescoes on the second floor. The palace is currently undergoing an extensive renovation and is to house the Old Masters' collection of the National Gallery from 2007.

Map
on page
18

THE NATIONAL GALLERY

Passing through the left gateway of the palace and taking a passage leading downhill, you will come to the **Sternberg Palace** (1700).

Since 1948 it has contained the most important section of the ★★★ **National Gallery ❹** (Národní galerie; Tues–Sun 10am–6pm; www.ngprague.cz). The Sternberg Gallery was founded in 1796 by the Society of Patriotic Friends of the Arts in Bohemia, a group of enlightened aristocrats determined to rouse Prague from its provincial stupor. The collection now comprises the National Gallery's Art of Antiquity and European Old Masters – the collection of European paintings of the 19th and 20th centuries is in Veletržní Palac *(see page 94)*. It's not a very large or balanced collection, but it does include some outstanding paintings, including Goya's *Portrait of Don Miguel de Ladizabal* (1815) and *Peter Burdett and his First Wife Hannah* by Joseph Wright of Derby (1765). The paintings below are described by provenance, not location.

Episcopal residence
Opposite the Schwarzenberg, and obscuring the National Gallery, lies the Archbishop's Palace ❸, built in 1550 and rebuilt several times in 1562–4, 1669–94, 1722–5 and 1764. Its present appearance dates from the last renovations, carried out during the reign of Maria Theresa.

Archbishop's palace guardian

DUTCH AND FLEMISH PAINTING

The gallery's holdings include works by most of the major Dutch and Flemish painters. Among the earliest works are a triptych depicting the *Adoration of the Magi* by Geertgen tot Sint Jans (1490–5), and *The Epitaph of Jan Cleemenssoen with the Well of Life* (1511) by the Master of the Well of Life. Just a little later, *Saint Luke Drawing the Virgin* by Jan Gossaert (*c.* 1513) shows the influence of the Italian Renaissance. There are also a number of works by the younger and elder Brueghels (*Village Scene* and *Winter Landscape*).

Later Dutch and Flemish works include an extensive collection of paintings by Peter Paul Rubens (1577–1640), notably the *Portrait of General Ambroggio Spinola* and *The Expulsion from the Garden of Eden*. Other outstanding works include the *The Scholar in His Study* by Rembrandt (1634), the *Portrait of Judge Jasper Schade van Westrum of Utrecht* by Frans Hals (1645), and Roelant Savery's *Garden of Eden* (1618).

ITALIAN PAINTING

The gallery has an important collection of works by the so-called Italian Primitives; it includes a triptych by Bernando Gaddi (*c.* 1330) and a *Lamentation* by Lorenzo Monaco (1408). The *Virgin with Four Saints and a Donor* (*c.* 1500) by Pasqualino Veneto is particularly fine. Of the later works, Bronzino's portrait of *Eleonora of Toledo* (1540–3) is a prized exhibit. Other notable later works include *St Jerome* by the Venetian painter Tintoretto (*c.* 1550), *The Annunciation to the Shepherds* by Bassano (*c.* 1575), and a number of paintings by Tiepolo (1696–1770).

Star Attraction
● **National Gallery**

GERMAN PAINTING

Perhaps the most impressive part of the Sternberg's collection is the display of German works. Notable among these are the two-sided *Hohenburg Altar* (1509) by Hans Holbein the Elder, a stunning manifestation of the northern Renaissance. Other outstanding works include the *Martyrdom of St Florian* (*c.* 1520) by Albrecht Altdorfer, and a fragment of an *Altarpiece* (*c.* 1520) by Lucas Cranach the Elder (more of which can be seen in the Castle Gallery). However, most famous of all is the large painting of the *Festival of the Rosary* (1506) by Albrecht Dürer, displayed opposite his *St Jerome in the Landscape.*

Festival of the Rosary *by Albrecht Dürer*

Map
on page
18

Final defenestration?
President Thomas Garrigue Masaryk's son, Jan, was a popular politician in his own right, and served as foreign minister in his father's cabinet between the wars. He became increasingly distrustful of Russia until the communists came to power in 1948, and just a few weeks after their takeover on 25 February, he fell to his death from a window in Czernin Palace, which remains the foreign ministry headquarters today. Whether he was pushed, or jumped, remains a mystery.

Loreto Church tower

TUSCANY PALACE

Leaving the National Gallery, continue past the Virgin's Column, created in 1720 by Ferdinand Maximilian Brokoff, to the far end of Hradčany Square; here you'll find the **Tuscany Palace ➎**, said to have been built in 1695 by Jean-Baptiste Mathey, the French architect whose work dominated Prague at the time. He was also responsible for the Church of the Crusader Knights *(see page 78)* and Troja Palace *(see page 93)*.

CZERNIN PALACE

Skirting to the left of the palace, you will come to Loreto Square (Loretánské náměstí), whose west side is dominated by the massive bulk of the **Czernín Palace** (not open to the public), which today houses the Foreign Ministry. Construction began at the end of the 1660s and continued over half a century. The palace, with its huge Corinthian columns, is evidence of the fascination which the *palazzi* of the Italian aristocracy held for Jan Humprecht Czernín, the Imperial ambassador to Venice. The architects commissioned to build the massive palace were for the most part famous Italian masters. The plans were drawn up by Francesco Caratti; their execution was entrusted to Giovanni Capuli, Giovanni Battista Maderna and Egidio Rossi, among others.

The Czernín were an old Bohemian family and their members had excelled time after time in the service of the Bohemian crown. The house in Prague was to become a 'Monumentum Czernin'. Its construction went on for several generations, until at last financial collapse put a stop to the project. After the palace had been partially destroyed by French troops in 1742, it was rebuilt and extended in 1747 by another architect, Anselmo Lurago. At the beginning of the 19th century the complex was used merely as a military barracks, but in 1928–32 it was restored once more, the work this time directed by a Bohemian architect, Pavel Janák. While the palace itself cannot be visited, its pleasant garden is open to the public from time to time in the summer months.

LORETO CHURCH

Opposite the Czernín Palace stands the **★★Loreto Church** ❻ (Tues–Sun 9am–12.15pm and 1–4.30pm), dedicated to the Virgin Mary and the most famous pilgrimage church in Prague. Construction of the church commenced soon after the Battle of the White Mountain in 1620, though the church's appearance dates mostly from the first third of the 18th century. The baroque façade was completed in 1721–5 and was the work of Christoph Dientzenhofer and his son Kilian Ignaz. The latter was also responsible for the forecourt adorned with angels in front of the entrance. In the tower hangs a glockenspiel of 27 bells, which was donated in 1694; every hour, the bells play a Czech hymn to the Virgin Mary.

Star Attraction
● **Loreto Church**

Below and bottom: frescoes in the Loreto cloister

CASA SANTA

The courtyard of the church is surrounded by a two-storey cloister (1634–1747). In the middle of it stands one of Prague's stranger monuments, a copy of the famous **Casa Santa** by Bramante, sculpted in 1626–31 by Giovanni Orsi. The original is in Loreto, in the Italian province of Ancona. According to the legend, angels supposedly transported the house of the Holy Family from Nazareth via Fiume to Loreto during the 13th

Map on page 18

century. The windowless, twilit interior was decorated in 1795 with a cycle of impressive frescoes.

Beside the Casa Santa stands a baroque fountain (1739–40) by Johann Michael Brüderle: *The Assumption of the Virgin Mary* (a replica). The 45 arches of the lower cloister were painted by Felix Anton Scheffler in 1750, with symbols from the *Litany of the Blessed Virgin*, a prayer of incantation. The six chapels house a number of remarkable works of art.

The Casa Santa

CHURCH OF THE NATIVITY

In the middle of the east wing, previously also the site of a chapel, now stands the **Church of the Nativity**, begun in 1717 by Christoph Dientzenhofer, continued by his son and finished by his stepson Georg Achbauer in 1734.

The interior is one of the most charming examples of Prague baroque art. A multitude of angels and cherubs, prophets, apostles and saints give the space a theatrical quality, the skilful use of light making some figures gleam more brightly than others. Of special interest are the exquisitely decorated organ (1734–8) and the three ceiling paintings: the *Presentation in the Temple* (1735) by Wenzel Lorenz Reiner beside the high altar, the *Adoration of the Shepherds* and the *Adoration of the Magi* (1742) by Johann Adam Schöpf.

Finally, a visit to the Treasury is well worthwhile, housed on the first floor of the entrance wing. It contains some 300 items of widely varying artistic merit. The highlight of the collection is the famous ★★ **Diamond Monstrance**, manufactured in Vienna in 1699 by a goldsmith named Künischbauer, and Stegner, a jeweller, possibly to a design by Johann Bernhard Fischer von Erlach. The monstrance weighs 12kg (26.4lbs) and is of gilded silver encrusted with 6,222 diamonds. Also worthy of note are the six other monstrances dating from 1673–1740. The collection also includes a Gothic chalice dating from 1510, a pacifical decorated with crystals and garnets dating from *c.* 1600, a home altar of silver (1650), crucifixes and mitres.

STRAHOV MONASTERY

From Loreto Square turn right by the Czernín Palace to Pohořelec (Place of the Fire), which at this point opens up to form a square. Take a small arched staircase at house No. 8 (or the main entrance, a little further to the west) which leads to the former ★★ **Strahov Monastery** (Strahovský klášter; www.strahovskyklaster.cz) ❼, one of the most famous sights in the city.

The Monastery of the Premonstratensians was founded in 1148 by Vladislav I, the King of Bohemia at the time. During the 16th–17th centuries, the complex was rebuilt, acquiring its present appearance at the end of the 18th century.

On the right is the library building; if you go up to the first floor, you will find the magnificent baroque rooms of the former **monastery library** (daily 9am–noon, 1–5pm).

PHILOSOPHER'S LIBRARY

You will first of all look through the entrance of the two-storey ★ **Philosophers' Library**, built in 1782–4 by Ignaz Palliardi, which measures 32m (105ft) long by 10m (33ft) wide and 14m (46ft) high. The main attraction, apart from the baroque bookcases, is the remarkable ceiling fresco, completed in 1794 in a period of only six months by

Star Attractions
- **Diamond Monstrance**
- **Strahov Monastery**

Below: Premonstratensian monks at Strahov
Bottom: the monastery

Below: inside the
Monastery Church
Bottom: ecclesiastical
emblems

Franz Anton Maulpertsch, Austria's most famous rococo artist; he was 70 years old when he and his assistant Marin Michl created this masterpiece.

Four great eras of mankind are depicted here, with a large number of identifiable individual figures. As you enter, along the length of the room are the Mythological Age (left) and the Age of Ancient Greece (left and right); on the short side opposite the entrance is the Christian Era. The end of the cycle, above the central section on the right-hand side, is represented by the Triumph of Heavenly Wisdom at the end of the world.

CURIOSITIES

The closest end of the corridor linking the two library rooms is lined with display cabinets of 'curiosities'. They are mostly specimens of marine creatures from a collection owned by Karel Jan Erben, and acquired by the monastery in 1798. One of the more bizarre pieces is a faked chimera.

The corridor linking the library to the second room houses medical, legal and scientific books. Also in the corridor is a facsimile of the famous *Strahov Gospel*, thought to have been written in about 800 in Trier. Four excellent portraits of the evangelists were added later, and date from about 900. Its magnificent binding dates from the 12th–17th centuries.

THEOLOGICAL LIBRARY

At the end of the corridor is the **Theological Library**. It was constructed in 1671–9 by Giovanni Domenico Orsi and extended by two arches in 1721. The magnificent ceiling frescoes were painted in 1723–7 by Siard Nosecký, a member of the monastery. Apart from the theological books, the room also houses 17th-century globes and glass cases displaying beautiful manuscripts.

THE STRAHOV COLLECTION OF ART

The **Picture Gallery** (Tues–Sun 9am–noon, 12.30 –5pm), upstairs above the monastery's cloister, are well worth a look. The works of art are mostly religious, but there are a number of secular works by baroque and rococo painters; these include Norbert Grund (1717–67) and Franz Anton Maulbertsch (1724–96).

One of the most important works owned by the monastery is the wooden Strahov Madonna, by a Czech sculptor, dating from the second third of the 14th century. There is also a wonderful *Judith* from the workshop of Lucas Cranach the Elder (1472–1553).

> **Precious manuscripts**
> Among the most precious manuscripts held at Strahov is the *Strahov Gospel*, the oldest manuscript in the collections. In addition the library holds the *Gerlaci Chronicon* codex dating from 1220; and a first-edition copy of Copernicus' groundbreaking work *De revolutionibus orbium coelestium* ('On the revolutions of the celestial orbs'). In this series of six volumes, Copernicus published his heliocentric theory of the structure of the universe.

CHURCH OF OUR LADY

From the monastery courtyard, turn left towards the main gate. On the left stands the former monastery Church of Our Lady, which developed from a Romanesque basilica and acquired its present appearance during the 17th–18th century. The baroque interior contains the tomb of the commander of the Imperial army, General Count Pappenheim, who died in the Battle of Lützen (1632). In 1787, Mozart played on the baroque organ here, which dates from 1740.

The Library Building near the church was built in 1782–4 by the Italian architect Palliardi in a style which marks the transition from late baroque to classicism. But the little Chapel of St Rochus near the main entrance is still predominantly Gothic in style, although it was built in 1603–11. It is used today as an exhibition hall.

Church of Our Lady sculpture

Map
on page
52

3: The Lesser Quarter

Malostranské náměstí – Waldstein Palace – Church of St Mary in Chains – Kampa Island

Extending from below Hradčany down to the Vltava, the Malá Strana is one of the oldest and most interesting parts of the city. After the Battle of the White Mountain (1620), at which the forces of the Protestant Union were defeated, it became the favoured residential area of the aristocracy which had remained loyal to the emperor; this explains why the district contains a large number of fine patrician mansions.

From Castle Hill, the Lesser Quarter and its focal point, the Lesser Quarter Square (Malostranské náměstí), can be reached via the Nové zámecké schody or by taking Nerudova *(see page 53)*. You will also come to the Malostranské náměstí by taking two right turns on the way downhill, traversing Valdštejnská and passing the Waldstein Palace *(see page 53)*. Malostranské náměstí can also be reached directly via the Charles Bridge by taking Mostecká.

LESSER QUARTER SQUARE

Malostranské náměstí (Lesser Quarter Square), the large, enclosed square at the heart of the Lesser Quarter, evolved during the 13th century, but was

The 'Water Man'

As you stroll about Kampa Island *(see page 55)*, be warned of one local legend that's rumoured to be especially dangerous to unsuspecting tourists. The 'Water Man' is an amphibious creature resembling a man, but with webbed fingers and a green complexion. He lurks just below the surface of the Vltava, and will reach out when least expected to drag humans under the water. It's said he is especially brave at night among drunken revelers.

Lesser Quarter Square

completely remodelled during the baroque era (17th–18th centuries). Since then it has been divided into two separate squares by the massive complex of St Nicholas' Church and the former Jesuit College; the modern name, Malostranské náměstí, applies to both but was not adopted until 1869.

ST NICHOLAS' CHURCH

On the north and east sides of the square are a number of elegant façades dating from the baroque and rococo eras, in some cases later additions to medieval buildings. Thus, the Lesser Quarter Town Hall (No. 22) dates from 1479, and No. 23 combines three narrow old houses dating from the 14th century – as does the house U Montágů (No. 18) on the north side.

The focal point of the square is ★★ **St Nicholas' Church** (Chrám sv. Mikuláše; daily 9am–5pm) ❽, the largest and most impressive baroque church in Prague. On the site of a Gothic church which had been dedicated in 1283 and demolished during the 17th century, Christoph Dientzenhofer built the nave and the façade in 1703–17; his son, Kilian Ignaz Dientzenhofer, added the choir, the dome and the tower in 1737–52. After his death, the belfry was completed by Anselmo Lurago by 1755. The church adjoins the Collegiate Building which was erected for the Jesuits in 1673–90 by Domenico Orsi de Orsini.

THE WEST FRONT

The west front of the church is divided into three sections and surmounted by a gable; it is decorated with statues of the patron saint, St Peter the Apostle and St Paul, as well as the founding saints of the Jesuit order, Ignatius Francisco Xavier, and the Fathers of the Church, Saints Ambrosius, Gregory, Jerome and Augustine.

Today, the interior is dominated by the vast choir, added by Kilian Ignaz Dientzenhofer to the nave designed by his father. The observation tower on Petřín Hill would fit inside the vast

Below: St Nicholas' Church
Bottom: the baroque interior

Map
below

dome, which is 75m (246ft) high and is supported
by four slanting pillars. The dome fresco, the
Celebration of the Holy Trinity, was painted by
Franz Xaver Palko in 1752–3.

The figures on the pillars of the intersection, the
work of Ignaz Platzer (1769), represent four eastern teachers of the church.

CEILING FRESCO

The dome fresco

The main attraction inside the church is without
doubt the vast ceiling fresco in the nave, painted
by the Viennese artist Johann Lukas Kracker in
1760–1. It covers an area of 1,500sq m (16,150sq
ft) and depicts the *Apotheosis of St Nicholas*. The
saint, who was Bishop of Myra in Asia Minor at
the beginning of the 4th century, is honoured as
the preserver of justice and the patron saint of
town administrations, merchants and seafarers.

The fresco shows the saint in the middle, surrounded by angels. Below is a triumphal arch
with the saint's tomb; on the right can be seen
the liberation of three Roman officers who had
been sentenced to death, and on the left is a
mythical landscape with merchants and sailors.

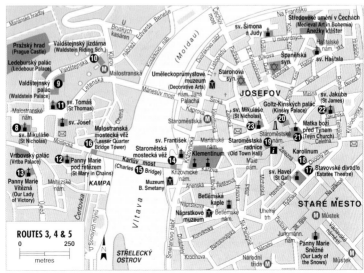

NERUDOVA

On the square in front of the church, also known as the Upper Square, stands a Trinity Column dating from 1715. Opposite is the Lichtenstein Palace (1791). Here begins **Nerudova**, the principal approach road to Hradčany.

The street, bordered by fine townhouses and mansions, has largely retained its historic appearance characteristic of the Prague high baroque era. In accordance with ancient custom, most of the houses bear names and painted signs: 'The Three Violins' (No. 12), 'St John Nepomuk' (No. 18), 'The Golden Horseshoe' (No. 33), 'The Black Madonna' (No. 36) and 'The Two Suns' (No. 47), which was the home of Czech writer Jan Neruda (1834–91), author of *Tales of the Lesser Quarter.*

The row of houses is interrupted by two magnificent baroque palaces: the Thun-Hohenstein Palace (No. 20 – today the Italian Embassy), erected in 1710–20 by Johann Blasius Santini-Aichel as the Kolowrat Palace – and the Czernin-Morzin Palace, the work of the same architect, built in 1713 and today the Romanian Embassy.

Neighbourhood gossip
When, in 1872, Jan Neruda wrote *Tales of the Lesser Quarter*, a collection of novellas and partly humourous, partly reflective sketches from the Malá Strana, he could hardly have envisioned the throngs of tourists pouring through the street that bears his name today: Nerudova, the main route to the castle. Neruda lived much of his life in No. 47, or 'The Two Suns' – which, in accordance with local tradition, was given a name and bore a corresponding sign.

The Two Suns

WALDSTEIN PALACE

It is worth making another detour from the Malostranské náměstí, this time in a northerly direction, to walk along Tomášská, to Waldstein Square (Valdštejnské náměstí). The right-hand side of the square is occupied by the **Waldstein Palace** ❾ (Sat and Sun 10am–4pm), the first major secular baroque building in Prague. After the Battle of the White Mountain in 1620, the general of the imperial army, Albrecht von Wallenstein, whose real name was Waldstein, purchased and demolished 23 houses on this site. On the land thus cleared he commissioned Italian architects to build the vast palace in 1623–30. The rooms open to the public include the mannerist/early-baroque main hall, with ceiling paintings by Baccio di Bianca, the Knights Hall with its 19th century leather wall covering, and the beautifully decorated circular audience chamber and mythological passage with its scenes from Ovid and Virgil.

Below: Waldstein
Palace door relief
Bottom: church of St Thomas

Well worth visiting are the ★ **Palace Gardens**
(May–Sept 9am–7pm, entrance on the Letenská).
Opening onto the garden is a magnificent log-
gia, known as the Sala Terrena, where concerts
are held during the spring and summer months.
A number of fine sculptures can be found in the
garden. The originals were the work of Adriaen
de Vries in 1622–6, but in 1648 they were cap-
tured as booty by Swedish soldiers, who occupied
the Lesser Quarter during the Thirty Years' War,
and taken to Drottningholm.

In 1914–15 they were replaced by copies.
Beginning at the Sala Terrena, there is a horse
on the left, followed by Venus and Adonis, Nep-
tune and Apollo. To the right is a second horse,
then a group of wrestlers, Laocoön and Bacchus.

VALDSTEJNSKA, TOMASSKA, JOSEFSKA...

Crossing the park or walking along Waldstein
Alley you will come to the former **Waldstein
Riding School ❿**. The fine building today houses
changing exhibitions.

Waldstein Alley (Valdštejnská) begins at Waldstein Square. On the left stand a number of lovely
mansions dating from the 18th century: the Lede-
bur Palace, rebuilt during the 19th century (No. 3)
with a charming terrace garden and a Sala Terrena
dating from 1716; the Kolowrat Palace (No. 10)
with a façade dating from 1784; and the Fürsten-
berg Palace (No. 14), built in 1743–7.

Returning along Tomašská, turn left at the
Lesser Quarter Square, following the tram lines,
into Josefská. On the left is the **Church of St
Thomas** (Kostel sv. Tomáše) ⓫. Founded in
1285 by Wenceslas II, the original Early Gothic
building was reconstructed in the baroque style
in 1725 by Kilian Ignaz Dientzenhofer, after it
had been struck by lightning.

Continuing right along Josefská, the Carmelite
Church of St Joseph (1673–92) is situated on the
left-hand side. Josefská leads to Bridge Street
(Mostecká), with the Kaunitz Palace (No. 15), a
lovely mansion with a rococo façade, built in 1773
by Anton Schmidt.

ST MARY IN CHAINS

A left turn into Mostecká, which links the Lesser Quarter Square with the Charles Bridge, followed by a right turn into Lázeňská, leads to the former Church of the Knights of Malta, the **Church of St Mary in Chains** (Kostel Panny Marie pod řetězem) **⑫** (the chains were used in the Middle Ages to close the gatehouse of the knights' monastery). The original 12th-century building was demolished and later building work was left unfinished. Only the choir was completed and now serves – separated from the main façade by the two 14th-century towers – as a church. It was renovated in 1640 and its main points of interest are the magnificent altars.

KAMPA ISLAND

Diagonally opposite stands the former Wolkenstein Palace (No. 11). To the left is the Great Priory Square (Velkopřevorské náměstí), with the baroque Great Priory Palace (No. 4), built in 1726–38, the adjoining Garden of the Knights of Malta and the Buquoy-Longueval Palace (No. 2), dating from 1682 and rebuilt in 1738.

Creating an extension of the square is a small bridge leading to **Kampa Island** (Ostrov Kampa), formed by a narrow branch of the Vltava, the **Devil's Canal** (Čertovka). It is pleasant to take

> **Museum Kampa**
>
> This museum (daily 10am–6pm) was opened in 2001 to house the collections of Jan and Meda Mladek, based around works by the Expressionist and Cubist sculptor Otto Gutfreund (1889– 1927) and the painter and designer František Kupka (1871–1963) who played an important part in the development of abstraction. As well as extensive galleries dedicated to these two artists, there are interesting displays of contemporary Bohemian art. The real star, however, is the building itself, an old mill converted by the architect Helena Bukovjanská, and topped by glass cube by Marian Kasměla. The glass bridge that looks over the Vltava is by Václav Cigler.

Kampa Island

Map
on page
52

Tiniest wonder
Housed in the Church of Our Lady of Victory, the Baby Jesus of Prague is known among the faithful as far away as Latin America. The 23-cm (9-inch) wax doll is famous for the miraculous powers it is said to possess, and thousands of pilgrims visit the 'Bambino di Praga' each year, offering prayers for their loved ones. Although its origins remain obscure, it has been in Prague since at least 1600. Caretakers change its clothes every day, and the Bambino's wardrobe boasts more than 70 ornate robes in all.

Maltese Cross

a short walk through its pretty gardens and past the old houses. There is a magnificent view of the Charles Bridge and the Old and New Towns from the river bank. In Kampa Park is **Museum Kampa** *(see box on previous page)*. the island suffered greatly during the floods of 2002, although now there is little sign of the devastation and most buildings have been reopened.

SQUARE OF THE KNIGHTS OF MALTA

After this detour return to Great Priory Square and the Church of St Mary in Chains, bearing left from there towards the **Square of the Knights of Malta** (Maltézské náměstí). Of particular note are the Statue of St John (1715) by Ferdinand Maximilian Brokoff, erected in thanks for the end of an epidemic of plague, the Old Post (No. 8) and – at the south end of the square – the former Nostitz Palace, built in 1658–60. In 1720 the façade was redesigned in the baroque style before acquiring its rococo features in 1770.

From the Maltézské náměstí, the Harantova leads back to Karmelitská, the main thoroughfare of the Lesser Quarter. To the left, there is another detour to Petřín Hill *(see page 90)*, from where there is a magnificent view of Prague.

OUR LADY OF VICTORY

Back towards the Lesser Quarter Square is the ★ **Church of Our Lady of Victory** (Chrám Panny Marie Vítězné) **⑬**, the city's earliest baroque church (1611–13; daily 8.30am–7pm). Originally it was Lutheran, and was given to the Carmelites in 1624, who re-dedicated it to Our Lady of Victory (after the Battle of the White Mountain). Inside the church, known for its fine altars, is the Baby Jesus of Prague, standing on the central side altar on the left *(see box above)*.

It is also well worth visiting the baroque terraced garden (*c.* 1720) of the **Vrtbovský Palace** (Karmelitská 25; daily, Apr–Oct 10am–6pm), which has fine views of the castle and the Lesser Quarter, and classical statues by Matthias Braun.

4: The Charles Bridge

One of Prague's loveliest and most characteristic sights is the Charles Bridge, which connects the Lesser Quarter with the Old Town. It also combines in unique fashion the original Gothic architecture with baroque sculpture.

The first stone bridge was constructed here during the second half of the 12th century, in the place of a 10th-century wooden bridge which was situated somewhat further to the north. Known as the Judith Bridge after the consort of King Vladislav I, it still exists today in the pillar foundations in the Vltava, and the smaller of the bridge towers on the Lesser Quarter side.

OLD TOWN BRIDGE TOWER

In 1342 the Judith Bridge collapsed. In 1357, Charles IV laid the foundation stone for the new, Gothic, construction. Building began under the supervision of the cathedral architect, Peter Parler, who was only 27 at the time. However, the bridge was not completed until 1399, after Parler's death in the same year.

Parler's last work was the magnificent **Old Town Bridge Tower** (Staroměstská mostecká věž) ⓮, which marks the entrance to the bridge. This vast construction, standing on the first bridge support,

Maps on pages 52 & 59

Below: lovers on the Bridge
Bottom: across the Vltava to the Old Town

Maps on pages 52 & 59

A drowned martyr

Prague is known not only for defenestrations, but for depontefications as well. In 1393, King Wenceslas IV learned that the Vicar General, John of Nepomuk, was organizing monks against his corrupt treatment of the church. The king had him thrown over the Charles Bridge, and according to legend a ring of seven stars appeared in the water where he sank. The martyr was later made a saint, and it's said that touching the relief of the death scene on his statue *(No. 15 on page 60)* will assure your return to Prague.

Statue of St John Nepomuk

is decorated with fine sculptures on its east side. High up, in a gallery of tracery, stand St Adalbert (left), the second bishop of Prague, and St Wenceslas (right). Below, in a rounded arch, is Charles IV (left); on a foreshortened representation of the Charles Bridge is St Vitus (centre) and finally Wenceslas IV (right). Further down again is a row with the coats of arms of the Holy Roman Empire (inside left), Bohemia (inside right) and the Luxembourg domains. Here – and elsewhere on the tower – is Wenceslas IV's personal emblem: a kingfisher in a 'love knot', a knotted handkerchief.

Equally elaborate sculptures on the bridge side of the tower were destroyed in 1648 during the Swedish occupation. A memorial plaque recalls the Thirty Years' War.

THE BRIDGE

Slightly curved, the ★★★ **Charles Bridge** (Karlův most) ⑮ is 510m (558 yards) long and 10m (33ft) wide. It spans the Vltava by means of 17 pillars, strengthened on both sides and forming 16 arches. It is one of Prague's main tourist thoroughfares, particularly in the summer when artists set up their stalls and buskers entertain. All is not well with the bridge, however, as the foundations are slowly crumbling and a reconstruction programme has now been started to save this medieval treasure.

During the Middle Ages the bridge had no sculptural decoration, relying for effect on its harmonious proportions and massive arches made of carefully worked stones, as well as on the towers at each end. The only adornment in those days was a crucifix (5), subsequently renewed on several occasions. The 30 statues adorning the bridge were added over a period of 250 years. Nonetheless, visually they form a harmonious whole in spite of their widely varying artistic merits. Many are replicas; the originals are now in the Lapidarium of the National Museum in Stromovka Park.

The first statue to be added to the bridge was that of St John of Nepomuk (15), which was placed near the point where John, the Vicar General and deputy bishop, who was canonised in

1729, was thrown into the Vltava and drowned in 1393 on the orders of Wenceslas IV *(see panel on facing page)*. Between 1706–14, a further 21 statues were erected on the bridge.

The most important baroque sculptors whose work can be seen here are Johann Brokoff (15), his son Ferdinand Maximilian Brokoff (4, 10, 14, 20, 23, 27, 28), and the accomplished Tyrolean artist Matthias Bernhard Braun (2, 16, 24).

Star Attraction
● **Charles Bridge**

BRIDGE STATUES

1 *The Virgin Mary with St Bernhard* (1709) by Matthias Wenzel Jäckel (replica).
2 *St Ivo* (1711; replica made in 1928) by Matthias Bernhard Braun.
3 *The Virgin with Ss Dominic and Thomas Aquinas* (1708; replica made in 1961) by Matthias Wenzel Jäckel.
4 *Ss Barbara, Margaret and Elizabeth* (1707) by Ferdinand Maximilian Brokoff.
5 Crucifixion group with a crucifix dating from 1629 and figures from 1861.
6 *Pietà* (1859) by Emanuel Max.
7 *St Anne with the Virgin Mary and Infant Jesus* (1707) by Matthias Wenzel Jäckel.
8 *St Joseph* (1854) by Emanuel Max.
9 *Ss Cyril and Methodius* (1928) by Karel Dvořák.
10 *St Francis Xavier* (1711; copy dating from 1913) by Ferdinand Maximilian Brokoff.
11 *St John the Baptist* (1857) by Josef Max.
12 *St Christopher* (1857) by Emanuel Max.
13 *Ss Wenceslas, Norbert and Sigismund* (1853) by Josef Max.
14 *St Francis Borgia* (1710) by Ferdinand Maximilian Brokoff.

The St Luitgard group

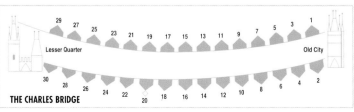

THE CHARLES BRIDGE

Map on page 59

Curious script

There's a tragic tale behind the golden Hebrew script on the bridge's crucifixion scene (5). The letters were added in 1696 after a show trial in which the local Jewish merchant Elias Backoffen was sentenced to death for 'debasing the Holy Cross'. The phrase surrounding Christ on the statue reads 'holy, holy, holy is our lord of the multitiude' – an important expression of faith in the Hebrew tradition – and was intended to humiliate the Jewish community.

Tourists at the Bridge Tower

15 *St John of Nepomuk* (1683); model by Johann Brokoff, reliefs by Matthias Rauchmüller, cast by W. Heroldt.

16 *St Ludmilla* (*c.* 1720) from the atelier of Matthias Bernhard Braun.

17 *St Anthony of Padua* (1707) by Johann Meyer.

18 *St Francis the Seraphic* (1855) by Emanuel Max.

19 *St Judas Thaddeus* (1708) by Johann Meyer.

20 *Ss Vincent of Ferrer and Procop* (1712) by Ferdinand Maximilian Brokoff. To the left, beneath the bridge, stands a late Gothic column with a statue of Roland (copy, 1884). The legendary hero of the *Song of Roland*, known in Czech as Brunsvík, who won the friendship of a lioness, is the patron of the bridge.

21 *St Augustine* (1708) by Johann Friedrich Kohl (copy).

22 *St Nicholas of Tolentino* (1708) by Johann Friedrich Kohl (copy).

23 *St Cajetan* (1709) by Ferdinand Maximilian Brokoff.

24 *St Luitgard* (1710) by Matthias Bernhard Braun (considered to be the sculpture with the greatest artistic merit and made when Braun was only 26).

25 *St Philip Benitius* (1714) by Michael Bernhard Mandl (copy).

26 *St Adalbert* (1709) by Joseph Michael Brokoff (copy).

27 *St Vitus* (1714) by Ferdinand Maximilian Brokoff.

28 *Ss John of Matha, Felix of Valois and Ivan* (1714) by Ferdinand Maximilian Brokoff (the figure of the Turk is particularly well-loved).

29 *Ss Cosmas and Damian* (1709) by Johann Meyer.

30 *St Wenceslas* (1858) by Joseph Kamill Böhm.

LESSER QUARTER BRIDGE TOWER

Lesser Quarter Bridge Tower ⓰: the tower on the left (south) side is a relic from the Judith Bridge (1158–72; *see page 57*). The right-hand (north) tower was erected later, in 1464.

5: Wenceslas Square to the Old Town Square

Estates Theatre – Karolinum – Old Town Hall – Old Town Square – Teyn Church – Church of St James – Church of St Nicholas

The Charles Bridge marks the beginning of the Old Town (Staré město), which can conveniently be visited following the tour of Hradčany and the Lesser Quarter. It is recommended, however, that at least one day be reserved for the visit to the Old Town. It is thus more practical to begin the tour at **Wenceslas Square** (Václavské náměstí), in the vicinity of which will be found many hotels and shops.

Star Attraction
● Estates Theatre

Below: Astronomical Clock detail, Old Town Hall
Bottom: the Estates Theatre

ESTATES THEATRE

From Václavské náměstí *(see page 81)*, take the narrow alley Na můstku at the far end, which leads into the Old Town. Before continuing straight ahead towards the Old Town Square, however, make a short detour by turning right into Rytířská, at the end of which stands the ★★ **Estates Theatre** (Stavovské divadlo) **17**. Renovated in 1990–1, this theatre was actually the first in the city. Built in 1781–3, it was inaugurated as the Nostitz Theatre on 21 April 1783 with a performance of Lessing's *Emilia Galotti*. On 29 October 1787 it was also the setting for the first

Map on page 52

performance of Mozart's *Don Giovanni*, which he had completed in Prague. From 1798 it was known as the Estates Theatre, and from the middle of the 19th century as the German National Theatre. After World War II it was named after the playwright and actor Josef Kajetán (1808–56), who worked here as a dramatist. It was during one of his comedies that today's Czech national anthem was heard for the first time. Today, plays and operas are performed here.

Below: detail of the house
'To the Two Bears'
Bottom: Karolinum fountain

THE KAROLINUM

Immediately on the left stands the **Karolinum** ⑱, the original building of the university founded in Prague by Charles IV in 1348, and thus the oldest university in Central Europe.

The building was based on a house constructed in about 1370 on this very site; all that remains today is a magnificent Gothic oriel window designed by the school of Peter Parler. The baroque façade dates from 1718 and was rebuilt in the neo-Gothic style; between 1934–50 it was restored in a way which was largely faithful to its original Gothic appearance.

From here you can continue directly to the Old Town Square, but a small detour is recommended. First bear left and follow Havelská to the Church of St Gallus (sv. Havel), originally Gothic but now

furnished with a fine baroque façade (1690–1700), then turn right into Melantrichova. On the corner of Kožná stands the house called 'To the Two Bears' (c. 1570), in which the 'roving reporter' Egon Erwin Kisch was born in 1885 and subsequently lived for many years.

OLD TOWN HALL

Melantrichova ends opposite the ★ **Old Town Hall** (Staroměstská radnice) ⓳ (Apr–Oct, Tues–Sun 9am–6pm, Mon 11am–6pm; Nov–Mar, Tues–Sun 9am–5pm, Mon 11am–5pm). Its history stretches back to 1338, when John of Luxembourg permitted the citizens of the 'old town of Prague' (in contrast to the 'Lesser Quarter') to convert their burghers' assembly hall into a town hall. The tower was added in 1364, followed in 1381 by the Gothic oriel chapel. The Late Gothic portal was built in about 1460; to the right is the astronomical clock. During the first half of the 16th century, a Renaissance-style extension was added to the left which has a fine triple window group and the inscription *Praga Caput Regni*. To the left, the adjoining building dates from 1897.

ASTRONOMICAL CLOCK

The famous ★★ **Astronomical Clock** consists of a calendar dial (at the bottom), a clock dial (above) and the Procession of Apostles (at the top), which was added during the 19th century. The calendar dial moves on one position at midnight every day; the signs of the zodiac and the representations of the months, with scenes from rural life, were painted by Josef Mánes in 1864–5 (these have now been replaced with replicas).

The clock dial marks, with Arabic figures round the outside of the face, the 24 hours from one sunset to the next; beneath, in Roman numbers, it indicates our modern time divisions. The circle above depicts the signs of the zodiac; a golden pointer indicates the month and the position and phase of the moon and the sun. Finally, 12 arched rays mark the nightly position of the planets.

Star Attraction
● Astronomical Clock

Stop watch
Legend has it that when the builder of the Astronomical Clock, Mikuláš of Kadaň, completed his masterpiece in the early 15th century, the king had his eyes stabbed out so he could never build another like it. Years later, as the old clockmaker was about to die, he asked the king's son to let him inside his beloved clock once more. The prince agreed, but once inside, the old man casually passed his hand once across the clock's gears and it ceased running for over a century.

Old Town Hall mosaic

Map on page 52

Map on page 52

Place of execution
The Old Town Square became the city's focal point for gatherings and executions. In 1437, 56 Hussite soldiers were put to death here, and on the order of Ferdinand II, the 27 leaders of the rebellion of 1618 were executed here on 21 June 1621: noblemen and ordinary citizens, Germans and Czechs (24 of them by a single executioner); crosses set in the ground and a plaque on the Town Hall recall the event.

Every hour, on the hour, the two windows above the clock face open to reveal the procession of the 12 apostles; six to the right and six to the left. Then the windows close once more, a cock crows tinnily, and Death turns the hourglass over and rings the death knell.

COUNCIL CHAMBER

It is possible to visit the interior of the Town Hall. From the Entrance Hall (with 19th-century mosaic pictures), the visitor enters the Late Gothic Council Chamber, with a magnificent beamed ceiling, coats of arms and symbols of the crafts guilds. A Renaissance portal (1619) leads into the new Assembly Chamber (1879); the two monumental paintings by Václav Brožík depict *Jan Hus before the Council in Constance* and *The Election of George of Podebrady as King of Bohemia*, which took place in 1458 in the Old Town Hall.

Finally, the visitor can enjoy the magnificent panorama from the Town Hall Tower, almost 70m (230ft) high (with a lift from the second floor).

OLD TOWN SQUARE

Leaving the Town Hall, you should turn left towards the spacious ★★**Old Town Square** (Staroměstské náměstí). On three sides it is enclosed by Gothic, Renaissance, baroque and rococo-style buildings, which form a harmonious unity despite the contrasting architectural styles. On the fourth (west) side, a neo-Gothic extension was added to the Town Hall in 1838–48, but it was destroyed during the May Uprising of 1945.

To the north of the square stands the imposing **Monument to Jan Hus**. It was the work of Ladislav Šaloun, and was erected on this spot in 1915 to mark the 500th anniversary of the death at the stake of the Czech reformer and religious hero Jan Hus in Constance.

To the right is a fine rococo building jutting out into the square. The former **Kinsky Palace 20** was built in 1755–65 by Anselmo Lurago to a design by Kilian Ignaz Dientzenhofer, who had

Old Town square façade

died before his plans could be realised. During the 19th century the palace housed a German grammar school attended by the writer Franz Kafka. The palace contains the Collection of Prints and Drawings of the National Gallery. Changing exhibitions are also held here (closed at present, *see* www.ngprague.cz).

Opposite the Old Town Hall, between Týnská and Celetná, stands the building which once housed the Teyn School, characterised by Romanesque cellar arches, a Late Gothic arcade and Renaissance gables.

TEYN CHURCH

Behind the former Teyn School, and accessible through a narrow passageway, is the ★★ **Teyn (or Týn) Church** (Matka boží před Týnem; open for mass and Mon–Fri 9am–noon, 1–2pm though tmimes are apt to change) ㉑. Its landmark 80-m (262-ft) towers dominate the Old Town. The characteristic Teyn gable (1463) is crowned by a gilt Madonna (1626).The present building was erected between 1365 and 1511 on the site of the 12th-century church of the Virgin Mary. There was a long interruption in the construction during the Hussite Wars. The North Tower, which was destroyed by fire in 1819, was restored to its original form in 1835.

Star Attractions
● Old Town Square
● Teyn Church

Below: Teyn Church
Bottom: the Kinsky Palace,
with the statue of Jan Hus

Map on page 52

Symbols of faith
King George of Podebrady (1458–71), the 'Hussite King', had a stone chalice covered with gold foil set into the gable niche between the two towers of the Teyn Church, as a symbol of the Hussite faith. After the Catholic victory at the Battle of the White Mountain (1620) it was replaced by a statue of the Virgin Mary; the Hussite chalice was melted down to make the crown, halo and sceptre.

Teyn Church interior

The unusually high interior was partly rebuilt in the baroque style following a fire during the 17th century. The first great Bohemian baroque artist, Karel Skréta (1610–74), painted the High Altar picture of *The Assumption of the Virgin Mary* and four side altars. The baroque vaulting was added in 1679, when the windows were also altered and the pillars added.

Also of interest are the older works of art, including the Altar of the Cross (1330–40) in the north aisle, a Gothic *Madonna* (c. 1400), the pewter Baptismal Font (1414) – the oldest in the city – the Late Gothic Pulpit (15th century), and the Stone Baldaquin (1493) above the grave of the Utraquist bishop Augustinus Lucianus.

By the last pillar on the right-hand side stands the marble tombstone of the Danish astronomer Tycho Brahe (1546–1601), who worked in Prague during the reign of Rudolf II. The scholar lost the tip of his nose in a duel or brawl and had to wear a silver prosthesis, which can be seen on the tombstone. To the right, in the aisle, stands the oldest pewter font in Prague; it dates from 1414.

CHURCH OF ST JAMES

Leave the church and skirt round the outside to the North Door (in Týnská), in order to study the magnificent tympanum (c. 1400), which depicts scenes from the Passion of Christ (the Scourging, the Crucifixion and the Crown of Thorns).

Passing through a handsome archway (1559–60) you will come to the **Teyn**. Newly renovated with boutiques, restaurants and offices, this is one of the oldest market places in the city, with a history stretching back to the 10th century.

Passing behind the church, continue on beneath the arches of the 13th-century **Customs House** and into the Ungelt Courtyard. You will eventually come to the **Church of St James** (Kostel sv. Jakuba) ㉒. Founded in 1232, the church was rebuilt in 1318–74 and renovated in the baroque style in 1689–1702. Of interest are the unusual reliefs on the façade, carved in 1690–1702 by the Italian sculptor Ottavio Mosta: St Francis (left),

St James (centre) and St Anthony (right). The reliefs are transformed into sculptures in some places; in others they seem to be buried in the wall. The baroque conversion of the interior was particularly successful. The three rows of arches in the choir are exceptionally fine. The impressive painting on the High Altar, the *Martyrdom of St James*, was painted by Wenzel Lorenz Reiner in 1739. Concerts are often held in the church.

Of note amongst the many other works of art in the church is the magnificent Tomb of Count Vratislav von Mitrowitz. Designed by Johann Bernhard Fischer von Erlach, it was executed in 1714–16 by Ferdinand Maximilian Brokoff. The dying Count is depicted in full battledress. To the right is Chronos, with a beard; to the left, the Angel of Glory, and below on the left stands the allegorical figure of Mourning.

HOUSE OF THE BLACK MADONNA

Leaving the Church of St James, you can either retrace your steps to the Old Town Square, or make a loop by following Celetná. The latter is one of the oldest streets in the city, though most of its houses were remodelled in the baroque style. At No. 34, at the corner of Celetná and Ovocný, is the ★ **House of the Black Madonna**, with a statue of the Black Madonna protected in a niche on the

Below: Black Madonna statue on the House of the Black Madonna in Celetná
Bottom: Church of St James – façade relief detail

Map on page 52

corner of the façade. Built in 1911–12 by Josef Gočár, and completely renovated in 1994, this important piece of modernist design is now the National Gallery's ★★ **Museum of Czech Cubism** (Tues–Sun 10am–6pm; www.ngprague.cz).

Church of St Nicholas

Once back at the Old Town Square, cross it diagonally towards the ★ **Church of St Nicholas** ㉓. Not to be confused with the church of the same name in the Lesser Quarter, and founded in 1272 by German merchants, the church was rebuilt in 1732–7 in the baroque style by Kilian Ignaz Dientzenhofer (1689–1751), the supreme master of the Bohemian late baroque style. It has a very chequered history: it once served as a warehouse, and in 1870–1914 as a Russian Orthodox church. Since 1920 it has belonged to the Czechoslovak Hussite Church, which was also founded here.

Today, the church seems an integral part of the Old Town Square, but until 1901 it was separated from the latter by the Krenn House, which jutted out into the square alongside the Town Hall. The imposing façade was designed to be surveyed in close-up, and approaching it you will get a good impression of the effect it must have created in times past. The sculptures are the work of Anton Braun, a nephew of the famous Matthias Braun.

Art nouveau street

If you head north from the the Old Town Square, the **Pařížská** (Paris Street) branches off towards the northwest. Created over a century ago, within the framework of an arbitrary restoration programme for the Josefov *(see page 71)*, its magnificent art nouveau façades make it the most spectacular street in the entire city.

The elegant Pařížska

Of particular interest, however, is the masterly arrangement of the interior, by means of which Dientzenhofer created an impressive dome section despite the relatively small area which the building occupies. The central area is enclosed by the choir and chapels. Larger-than-life-size statues of saints by Anton Braun, and frescoes by the Bavarian artist Peter Asam the Elder, adorn the cupola. The copious stucco is the work of Bernardo Spinetti. The large chandelier was commissioned by the Russian Orthodox church at the end of the 19th century from the Bohemian glass-blowing factory in Harrachov.

KAFKA'S BIRTHPLACE

A building standing to the left of the church served as a monastery until 1785. Until the middle of the 19th century it was used as an archive and then as a theatre. When the house, known as The Tower, was rebuilt here on the corner of the Maiselova, a doorway from the damaged building was incorporated. As the modern plaque recalls, the writer Franz Kafka was born here on 3 July 1883. The house is now a small museum.

MUSEUM OF DECORATIVE ART

From here, Kaprova leads down to the Vltava; famous due to the novel *The House in the Kaprova*, written by M.Y. Ben-Graviel and subsequently filmed. A right turn into Maiselova leads to the former Jewish Quarter *(see page 70)*, but Kaprova runs down to the broad 17 Listopadu (17 November Street), in which the ★★**Museum of Decorative Art** (Tues–Sun 10am–6pm) at No. 2 is well worth a visit. The museum building, built in Neo-Renaissance style and completed in 1901, backs onto the Old Jewish Cemetery *(see page 74)*. The stylish permanent galleries were opened in 2000, with particularly impressive displays of late-19th and 20th century costume, and Czech graphic art. The are also fine collections of Bohemian and Venetian glass, porcelain, timepieces, tapestries and furniture.

Star Attractions
● **Museum of Czech Cubism**
● **Museum of Decorative Art**

Below: St Nicholas interior
Bottom: the square where Kafka was born

Map
on page
72

Object of fascination
The figure of the Golem has fascinated many authors, including Franz Kafka. The best book about the creature, *Der Golem*, was written by the Bavarian writer Gustav Meyrink, who spent many years in Prague. Its surreal, nightmarish atmosphere has also been adapted into a great film of the same name.

Rabbi Loew's grave

6: The Jewish Quarter

The earliest mention of Prague's Jewish community comes from a document by the Jewish merchant Abraham ben Jakob dated 965. The ghetto, or **Jewish Quarter** (Josefov) ❷, built in about 1100 and surrounded by a wall, soon became one of the largest Jewish communities in Europe. The major buildings of the Jewish Quarter collectively form the **Jewish Museum in Prague** (Nov–Mar: Sun–Fri 9am–4.30pm; Apr–Oct: 9am–6pm; closed on Jewish holidays; www.jewishmuseum.cz). Although Jewish Quarter suffered badly during the floods of 2002, all the sites have now re-opened.

THE GOLEM

Under Ferdinand I (1526–64), there were a number of acts of violence directed against Jews; in 1541 they were banned from the country, and only 15 Jewish families remained in Prague. But under the tolerant emperors Maximilian II (1563–76) and Rudolf II (1576–1612), the ghetto expanded to a total of over 7,000 inhabitants. However, the 16th century was a difficult time in the Jewish Quarter. The community was harrassed to such an extent that a myth was born out of their need for protection: The Golem.

According to the story, one Rabbi Loew, employing occult powers he had learned from studying the *Kabbal*, created a man-shaped creature out of the mud of the Vltava river, and when he placed a *shem* – a clay tablet inscribed with the name of God – in the Golem's mouth, it came to life. The Golem helped the Rabbi's people for a time, doing chores and odd jobs as well as defending their homes. But Rabbi Loew had to carefully remove the *shem* each Friday at sundown in honour of the Sabbath. When he forgot to do this one week, the Golem ran amock, destroying entire city blocks, until the Rabbi regretfully removed the *shem* for the last time and dismantled the creature.

If you're wondering whatever became of the Golem, locals will tell you that its dismantled remains are stored to this day in the attic of the Jewish Quarter's Old-New Synagogue. Although it has apparently lain dormant for centuries, legends say that it will rise again to defend the community in times of need.

EDICT OF TOLERANCE

After 1848, the ghetto became the fifth district of the provincial capital. It was christened Josefov (Joseph's Town) in honour of Joseph II (1780–90), who had issued the Edict of Tolerance in favour of the Jews. During the 19th century, the sanitary conditions became progressively more intolerable: there were neither water mains nor sanitation, and the number of typhus and cholera cases rose dramatically. In 1893, a programme of urban development began: block by block, the houses were pulled down and replaced by new buildings in the style of the time. Only six of an original total of 17 synagogues remained, plus the Jewish Town Hall and the Old Jewish Cemetery.

JEWISH ARTEFACTS

Before the German invasion (1939), almost 40,000 Jews lived in Prague; during the course of the war, more than 36,000 of them were murdered by the Nazis in concentration camps.

Below: Jewish Town Hall
Bottom: on the wall of the Ceremonial Hall

It was Hitler's intention to establish a major Jewish museum in Prague following his 'Final Victory'. It was to be the museum of an extinct race, and so he issued instructions to the 153 Jewish communities of the Protectorate of Bohemia and Moravia to provide Jewish handicrafts, ritual objects, books and documents, which thus escaped destruction and today form the most valuable collection of its kind in the world.

Silver treasure in the Maisel Synagogue

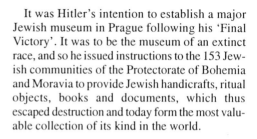

MAISEL SYNAGOGUE

Following Maiselova, the first important building is the former **Maisel Synagogue** (Maiselova synagóga) **A**. Constructed in 1590–2 as a triple-naved Renaissance edifice, the synagogue was rebuilt in 1893–1905 in the Neo-Gothic style. It houses an exhibition of the History of the Jews from the Establishment of Jewish Settlements to the Emancipation (up to the Renaissance).

JEWISH TOWN HALL

On the next corner but one is the **Jewish Town Hall** (Židovská radnice) **B**. Constructed in 1763 and adorned with a wooden tower at about the same time, the synagogue has a Jewish clock; its hands run in the opposite direction. Today, the building houses the Senior Rabbinical Council and the administrative offices and assembly chambers of the Jewish community, as well as a kosher restaurant.

Beside the Town Hall is the **Town Hall Synagogue** (Vysoká synagóga) **C**, also known as the High Synagogue, with a rectangular Renaissance Assembly Room.

OLD-NEW SYNAGOGUE

Opposite stands the most important architectural monument in the former Jewish Quarter: the ★★**Old-New Synagogue** (Staronová synagóga; not part of the Jewish Museum, *see* www.kehilaprag.cz) **D**. It was built in 1270 in the Early Gothic

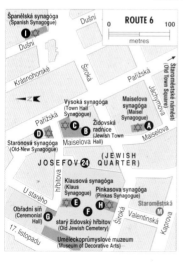

style, and is thus the oldest remaining synagogue in Europe in which services are still held. A huge banner used to hang from the vaulted ceiling; it was presented to the Jews of Prague by Emperor Ferdinand III in recognition of their bravery during the fierce Swedish siege of 1648.

The synagogue's entrance lobby, a 14th-century addition, had two tills which were used by the tax collectors. From here, women would pass through to the corridors reserved for them, from which they could follow the proceedings in the synagogue through openings in the wall. The synagogue itself was reached through a narrow doorway whose tympanum is decorated with an unusual representation of the Tree of Life.

Inside, the most notable features are the five-section rib vaulting supported by two octagonal pillars; the altar with the Torah shrine on the east wall; the pulpit surrounded by a hand-made, wrought iron balustrade (15th century).

Outside on the left, at the far end of U starého hřbitova (the Old Cemetery Alley) stands the **Klausen Synagogue** (Klausová synagóga) **E**, a baroque building dating from the end of the 17th century. It was erected on the site of three smaller buildings (a school, a hospital and a prayer hall) and was rebuilt at the end of the 19th century. Today, the Klausen houses a permanent exhibition on Jewish Customs and Traditions.

Star Attraction
● Old-New Synagogue

Below: Old-New Synagogue
Bottom: Old Jewish Cemetery

Map on page 72

OLD JEWISH CEMETERY

Near the synagogue is the entrance to the ★★★ **Old Jewish Cemetery** (Starý židovský hřbitov) **F**, established early in the 15th century; the oldest gravestone visible today is dated 1439, the most recent 1787, after which Joseph II forbade burials within densely populated districts of the city. The exact number of gravestones, many of which have disintegrated or sunk into the ground, is unknown, but is estimated to be at least 12,000. Over the centuries, however, it is thought that as many as 200,000 people were buried here. Here, too, is the grave of the Jewish scholar David Oppenheimer (died 1736), an ancestor of Robert Oppenheimer, inventor of the atomic bomb. Near the entrance stands the former **Ceremonial Hall** (Obřadní síň) of the Funeral Brotherhood **G**, which holds part of the exhibition on Jewish Customs and Traditions.

The Rabbi's grave

The most visited grave in the cemetery is that of Rabbi Loew (died 1609), which is at the far side of the cemetery, straight opposite the entrance. The Rabbi is remembered for using his occult powers to create the famous Golem out of clay, and then bringing it to life *(see page 70)*.

PINKAS SYNAGOGUE

In Široká is the **Pinkas Synagogue** (Pinkasova synagóga) **H**, which dates from the 12th century but which was subsequently rebuilt on several occasions. Since 1958 it has served as a poignant memorial to the 77,297 Jews from Bohemia and Moravia who were killed by the Nazis during World War II. Their names are inscribed in alphabetical order around the bare white walls. On the far wall are the names of the notorious death camps. The first floor contains powerful and moving drawings by children in the Theresienstadt (Terezín) concentration camp

In order to see the last synagogue, retrace your steps along U starého hřbitova alley, turning right at the end into Pařížská. The first road on the left (Široká) passes the **Spanish Synagogue** (Španělská synagóga) **I**. Built in 1882–93, it has a square ground plan and a mighty dome. The style is mock-Moorish, which accounts for its name. The exhibition here deals with the history of the Jews of Prague from the Emancipation to the Present Day. On the upper floor there is a display of Bohemian and Moravian synagogue silver.

Ceremonial Hall and the Decorative Arts Museum

7: The Southwest Section of the Old Town

Small Square – Clam-Gallas Palace – Klementinum – Square of the Crusader Knights – Smetana Museum – Bethlehem Chapel

Depending upon whether you approach this section of the Old Town from the Old Town Square, from Wenceslas Square or from the Charles Bridge, you will come across the sights described below in a different order, and will head for a different orientation point in each case. Those who choose to walk from the Old Town Square to the Charles Bridge (or vice versa) can take the **Karlova** and visit the other sights by means of short side-trips or detours. Or the walk could be turned into a round trip.

This route does not therefore describe a fixed itinerary. The individual sights are listed according to their location, beginning with the Karlova and then describing those which lie to the south, working from west to east.

SMALL SQUARE

The historic **Small Square** (Malé náměstí) behind the Town Hall, together with the arcades of U radnice (Town Hall Alley) which adjoins it to the north, form one of the most charming sections of

Map on page 76

Star Attractions
● **Old Jewish Cemetery**
● **Klementinum (overleaf)**

Below: Clam-Gallas Palace
Bottom: view over the Klementinum

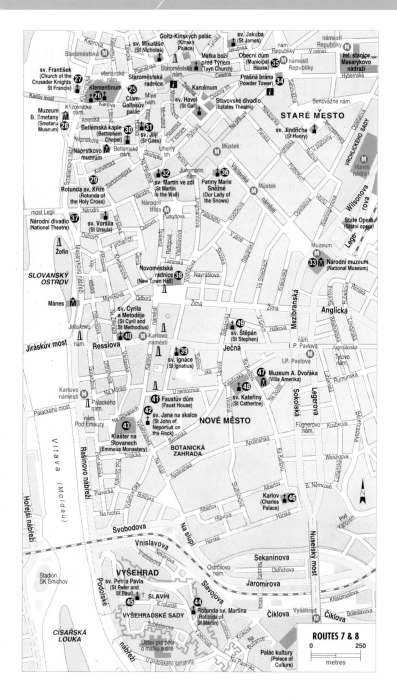

Map opposite

the Old Town. The arcades were built during the 14th century; the fountain in the middle, which boasts a fine Renaissance grating, dates from 1550. Many of the houses still bear their old names and signs. Of particular interest is No. 12, The Golden Lily, which was built by Christoph Dientzenhofer in 1698, and the house, 'To the Minute', which juts out and forms a link with the Old Town Hall. The latter was built in about 1600 in the Renaissance style and is decorated with attractive *sgraffito* painting.

The **Clam-Gallas Palace** (Clam-Gallasův palác) ㉕, on the corner of Karlova and Husova, is one of the most important baroque buildings in Prague. It was built from 1715 to plans drawn up by Johann Bernhard Fischer von Erlach. The main doorway is supported by statues of four giants which, together with the additional sculptural decoration, is the work of Matthias Braun. The ceiling fresco inside, which depicts *The Gods on Mount Olympus*, is by Carlo Carlone. Today the building serves as the city archive.

KLEMENTINUM

The ★★ **Klementinum** ㉖, the famous former Jesuit College, forms the largest complex of buildings in Prague after the castle. The original Dominican monastery on this site was founded during the 13th century but was almost completely destroyed during the Hussite Wars. In 1555, under the direction of the Jesuit Petrus Canisius, work commenced on a complex which was to serve as a Catholic bastion against the Protestant tendencies of Charles University.

The building itself, however, did not really get under way until 1578, when the foundation stone was laid for the Church of the Redeemer *(see page 78)*, Prague's first Jesuit church. The college building was erected between 1653 and 1722; it is centred around five courtyards, with study rooms and lecture theatres, libraries, an observatory and residential wings. Four libraries are housed on the premises, including the National Library and the University Library.

The tower and library

Dating from 1722, the Klementinum's baroque library hall was commissioned by the Jesuits and handed over to the university in 1773. The impressive space holds a collection of valuable books on philosophy and theology. Above the library is the astronomical tower, also built in the 1720s. Its main attraction is the wonderful view of the city from its balcony. Halfway up you can see the Prague meridian; when sunlight crossed the line at noon, a flag was hung from the tower. (Mar–Dec: Mon–Fri 2–8pm, Sat–Sun 10am–8pm; by guided tour only starting on the hour.)

The Observatory Tower

Map on page 76

Wonders of wine
While Bohemian wines can be quite fine, the region's finest vintages come from Moravia, in the eastern part of the country, where the gently rolling hills give the vineyards the best light. A good bet for picking up a souvenir bottle is the National Wine Bank, around the corner from the Square of the Crusader Knights at Křižovnická 22. The friendly staff will gladly help you choose according to your taste. Open daily except Sundays 10am–6pm.

Along the Karlova

CHURCH OF THE REDEEMER

Four churches are incorporated into the complex. Approached from the Old Town Square along **Karlova**, the first one is the Church of St Clement, built in 1711–15, which has a remarkable interior with eight baroque statues by Matthias Braun. It is followed by the round Welsh Chapel (1590–1600) and – opposite the Old Town Bridge Tower – the **Church of the Redeemer**. This was begun in 1578 and extended in 1643 by a triple-arched porch (with statues by Johann Georg Bendl dating from 1660) and a baroque style interior. In the northeast courtyard stands the Mirror Chapel, dating from 1724, in which concerts are held.

SQUARE OF THE CRUSADER KNIGHTS

As a result of its attractive architecture and its magnificent view across the Vltava to Hradčany, the charming **Square of the Crusader Knights** (Křižovnické náměstí) has become one of the most popular attractions in the Old Town.

The eastern boundary of the Klementinum is formed by the Church of the Redeemer; the northern one by the **Church of the Crusader Knights** ㉗, also known as the Church of St Francis, as it is dedicated to St Francis Seraph. The church used to belong to the monastery of the Order of the Knights of the Cross with the Red Star. Founded in 1237, this was the sole Bohemian knightly order at the time of the crusades. Its Grand Masters were the archbishops of Prague between 1561–1694, and were almost permanently at loggerheads with the Jesuits.

It was thus intended that the church, built in 1679–89 in accordance with the plans of the French architect Jean-Baptiste Mathey, should be equally as imposing as the Jesuit complex.

The interior of the church is of interest above all for the vast fresco in the dome; painted by Wenzel Lorenz Reiner in 1722, it portrays *The Last Judgment*. There is also a fine Gloriole (1702) by Matthäus Wenzel Jäckel above the High Altar. Outside, by the right-hand corner of the building, stands the Vintners Column with a statue of St Wenceslas (1676) by Johann Georg Bendel. In front of the church is a neo-Gothic bronze statue of Charles IV (1848) by the Dresden sculptor Ernst Hähnel.

Star Attraction
● Bethlehem Chapel

SMETANA MUSEUM

The ★**Smetana Museum** ㉘ (Muzeum B. Smetany; Wed–Mon 10am–noon, 12.30pm–5pm; www.nm.cz), Novotného lávka 1, is tucked away in a little street jutting out into the Vltava. In this house, decorated with *sgraffito* painting, there is a wealth of exhibits illustrating the life and works of the famous Czech composer Bedřich Smetana (1824–84). During the 2002 floods this museum suffered greatly, and many valuable manuscripts were damaged or destroyed.

Below: plaque at the Smetana Museum
Bottom: inside the Church of the Crusader Knights

Although not the oldest, the **Rotunda of the Holy Cross** (Rotunda sv. Kříže) ㉙, nearby on Konviktská ulice, erected in about 1100, is undoubtedly the loveliest of the three remaining Romanesque round churches in Prague.

BETHLEHEM CHAPEL

The ★★**Bethlehem Chapel** (Betlémská kaple; daily 9am–5pm) ㉚ is one of the most important sacred monuments in the country. The building

Map on page 76

Living gallery
One of the most prominent living Czech artists, Jiří Koláři is best known for his work with collage and his 'visual poems'. Koláři and his wife have opened their own gallery, Galerie Jiřího a Běly Kolářovi at Betlémské nám. 14, where you'll find the artist's own work as well as sculptures and paintings by up-and-coming local artists. Souvenir books featuring the work of prominent Czech artists are also available. Open daily 9am–6pm.

dates from 1391; it was here that Jan Hus preached from 1402 until shortly before he moved to Constance (1415). So, too, did Thomas Münzer a few years later, in 1521. Taken over by the Jesuits in the 17th century, after Protestantism was banned, the chapel was rebuilt, but then demolished in 1786. It was meticulously reconstructed in its original form in 1950–4, partly making use of original building materials. Memorabilia is on display in the adjoining rooms, where Hus lived.

Across the square is the ★★ **Náprstek Museum of Asian, African and American Cultures**, the archaeological and ethnographic departments of the National Museum (Tues–Sun 9am–5.30pm; www.aconet.cz/npm). The Asian collections are held in Liběchov Castle near Mělník, 32 km/20 miles north of Prague (closed at present for renovation). However, the holdings on display in Prague are impressive. They include substantial displays of Oceanic artefacts, pieces collected from 19th-century expeditions to southern and northern Africa, as well as a large ethnographic collection of items made by indigenous Amazonian peoples.

CHURCH OF ST GILES

Church of St Giles

The **Church of St Giles** (Kostel sv. Jiljí) ③①, also a Hussite place of worship, is a powerful Gothic building, constructed in 1339–71. In 1733 it was rebuilt in the baroque style, probably to plans drawn up by Kilian Ignaz Dientzenhofer. The ceiling frescoes were painted by Wenzel Lorenz Reiner. The interior is dominated by six massive columns dating from the Gothic era; during the 18th century they were clad in reddish-brown marble stucco and adorned with golden capitals.

The **Church of St Martin in the Wall** (Kostel sv. Martina ve zdi) ③②, Martinská ulice, was founded in 1178 and later incorporated into the city wall. The church is important for its historical significance, for it was here, in 1414, that Holy Communion 'in both kinds' (bread and wine) was offered for the very first time. Furthermore, various members of the famous family of sculptors, the Brokoffs, are buried here.

8: The New Town to Vysehrad

Wenceslas Square – National Museum – Powder Tower – Municipal House – Church of Our Lady of the Snows – National Theatre – Charles Square – Church of St Carlo Borromeo – Emmaus Monastery – Vyšehrad

The focal point of the New Town (Nové Město) is ★★ **Wenceslas Square** (Václavské náměstí). Laid out in 1348 by Charles IV as the Horse Fair in the centre of his New Town, which he himself had established, Wenceslas Square measured the same then as today: 750m (820yds) long, and only 60m (65yds) wide, giving it something of the appearance of a street. Closed to most motor traffic, the square is the city's favourite place for a stroll. Nowhere else will you find so many hotels, restaurants, shops, cinemas, cafés, bars and night-clubs as here. Many are hidden away in passage-ways or houses with public thoroughfares.

NATIONAL MUSEUM

At the top end of the square, forming a monu-mental boundary, is ★★ **National Museum** (Národní muzeum) ❸❸, built in 1885–90 in a neo-Renaissance style (daily, May–Sept 10am–6pm; Oct–Mar 9am–5pm; closed first Tues in the month; www.nm.cz).

Star Attractions
● Náprstek Museum
● Wenceslas Square
● National Museum

Wenceslas Square and statue

Map on page 76

Below: the State Opera, close to the National Museum
Bottom: the main staircase in the National Museum

The entire external and internal design was planned with the intention of creating here the intellectual centre of the nation, and thus includes vast sculptures and paintings portraying the most important events in the country's history: the galleries are grouped around a Hall of Fame surmounted by a vast dome. The galleries themselves are showing their age and the displays are, for the most part, a long series of dark cabinets. However, the mineral galleries are impressive and include a large collection of meteorites. Of the other displays, the archaeological section has some fascinating exhibits (the labelling is in Czech), and there is the usual depressing array of stuffed animals.

In 1912, following 30 years of preparatory work, the **Monument to St Wenceslas**, by the sculptor Josef Myslbek, was erected in front of the museum. It is considered to be a supreme example of the artistic style of the time. To the left of the museum stands the steel-and-glass old Federal Assembly building, currently home to Radio Free Europe and surrounded by armed guards.

FROM THE SQUARE TO PANSKA

In the middle of Wenceslas Square is a memorial to the student Jan Palach, who in January 1969 committed suicide by setting fire to himself as a protest against the August 1968 invasion.

At the lower end of the square, turn right into the main street **Na příkopě**, whose name recalls the fact that it was laid out along the former moat between the Old and the New Town, which was filled in 1781. On the right is the Sylvia-Tarouca Palace (No. 12), built in 1670 and reconstructed in 1748; then, on the corner of Panská, the Church of the Holy Cross dating from 1816. Finally, No. 22 is the Příchovský Palace, built in the 18th century and from 1875 known as the German House, now renamed the Slovanský dům (Slavic House).

On Panská itself is the ★ **Mucha Museum** (daily 10am–6pm; www.mucha.cz) dedicated to the life and work of the Czech art nouveau artist, Alphonse Mucha (1860–1939). Here you can see examples of his posters of Sarah Bernhard, and a number of his less-well-known oil paintings.

POWDER TOWER

A little further on to the left is the **Powder Tower** (Prašná brána) ㉞, built in 1475 by Mattias Rejsek as the East Gate of the Old Town. Here, near the Royal Court *(see below)*, began the Royal Way, along which the coronation procession of the kings of Bohemia passed on their way to Hradšany. The route led along the Celetná, across the Old Town Square, the Charles Bridge and the Lesser Quarter Square and up to St Vitus' Cathedral. In 1757, during the Seven Years' War, the tower was attacked by the Prussians and badly damaged: in 1875–86 it was rebuilt in neo-Gothic style. Inside can be seen parts of the original form. The tower, which affords a fine view of the city, received its present name during the 18th century, when gunpowder was stored here.

MUNICIPAL HOUSE

The tower is directly linked to the ★★ **Municipal House** (Obecní dům) ㉝, built in 1906–11 in art nouveau style on the site occupied between 1380–1547 by the Royal Court, the king's city residence, at the time more important than Hradčany. It was here that the Czechoslovak Republic was

Star Attraction
● Municipal House

Hotel Europa
On Wenceslas Square there are a number of art nouveau buildings (including the Palais Alfa, Peterka House and the Palais Koruna), but perhaps the most impressive is that of the Hotel Europa. It was built in 1903–6 by the Czech architects Drýak and Bendelmayer. Although you may not want to stay unless you are seeking out a taste of Prague's Stalinist era, it is well worth visiting the wonderfully decorated ground floor café.

Municipal House

Map
on page
76

Rebel stronghold
The Church of Our Lady of the Snows played a significant role in Czech history: from here, the Hussite preacher Jan Želivský and his followers set off to march to the New Town Hall *(see page 86)*, an act which led to the First Defenestration of Prague and the start of the Hussite Wars.

Our Lady of the Snows

proclaimed on 28 October 1918. The Municipal House has splendid interior decorations, and is home to the Prague Symphony Orchestra.

CHURCH OF OUR LADY OF THE SNOWS

Returning along Na příkopě to Wenceslas Square, the route continues along 28 October Street (Ulice 28. října). A short distance on the left is Jungmann Square (Jungmannovo náměstí), named after the Czech linguist and Enlightenment scholar, Josef Jungmann (1773–1847).

Here you should pass directly through the gateway of the Franciscan Presbytery to the ★ **Church of Our Lady of the Snows** (Kostel Panny Marie Sněžné) ㊱, one of the most interesting Gothic churches in Prague. Founded in 1347 by Charles IV, it was originally planned to be even larger than St Vitus' Cathedral. During the Hussite Wars, however, building came to a standstill. The choir, the only part of the building to have been completed by that time, collapsed during the 16th century; in 1601 it was rebuilt to its original height of 35m (115ft). No one can fail to be impressed by the sheer height of the single-nave, pillarless interior. The most important feature is the High Altar: created from 1625 onwards by several artists, it is the largest altar in the city.

NATIONAL THEATRE

If you continue from Jungmann Square along the same street, which is now known as Národní třída (National Street), you will arrive in front of the ★★ **National Theatre** (Národní divadlo) ㊲ *(see page 111)* on the banks of the Vltava.

The building represents the supreme achievement of 19th-century Bohemian architecture. Building began in 1868, and was financed entirely by private donations from the Czech people. Designed by Josef Zítek, the theatre was inaugurated on 15 June 1881 with a performance of Smetana's *Libuše*. Two months later it was burned to the ground, but was restored with the aid of endowments and donations. It re-opened in 1883.

Like the National Museum, which was built somewhat later, the National Theatre was planned from the start as a symbol of the revived Czech national awareness, and as a counterbalance to the city's numerous German-speaking theatres. The sculptures and paintings were planned with this aim in mind.

Star Attraction
● **National Theatre**

SLAVIC ISLAND

From this point, the Most Legií vítězná (Bridge of Legions) leads across the Vltava to join Vítězná Street. Turning south along the esplanade, however, leads to the setting of the Slavic Congress in 1848: the Slavic Island (Slovanský ostrov). The island is also known as Sophie Island because it is the setting for the **Sophie Concert Hall**, where, among other great luminaries, Berlioz, Liszt and Wagner performed. At the far end of the island is the Functionalist **Mánes House** (1927–30).

Shortly before reaching the end of the island, turn left into the Myslíkova ulice, following the direction of the tram lines, before forking diagonally right into Odborů and continuing to **Charles Square** (Karlovo náměstí), which – like Wenceslas Square – was laid out by Charles IV in 1348, but this one was to be the city's cattle market. It has retained its original proportions: 530m (580yds) by 150m (164yds).

Below: Sophie Concert Hall
Bottom: National Theatre

Map
on page
76

Memorial museum

On 18 June 1942, the Church of St Carlo Borromeo was the scene of an unequal struggle between the assassins of Reichsprotektor Heydrich and the SS. The assassins, who had hidden in the crypt, were betrayed, and the SS surrounded the church with 350 men. Despite their efforts, it took them six hours to force their way in, at the cost of 14 lives and dozens of injuries. But they failed to take a single captive because everyone had either been killed or committed suicide. Today, the crypt is a memorial museum, decorated with photos, documents and memorabilia (Tues–Sun; May–Sept 10am–5pm, Oct–Apr 10am–4pm).

Memorial at the Church of St Carlo Borromeo

NEW TOWN HALL

On the north side stands the **New Town Hall** (Novoměstská radnice) 🏳, also of historic interest. Built in 1374–1498 in Gothic style, the Town Hall was rebuilt in Renaissance style in 1526 and then reconstructed in 1900. This was the arena for the First Defenestration of Prague on 30 July 1419. Led by the Premonstratensian priest Jan Zelivský, a procession of Hussite supporters gathered at the Church of Our Lady of the Snows with the intention of demanding the release from prison of their fellow-Hussites. When their request was greeted with scorn (some say also with stones), the enraged crowd threw the town councillors from the window and lynched them. This incident provoked the outbreak of the Hussite Wars, which were to continue for 15 years.

TWO INTERESTING CHURCHES

In the southern section of the square, the east side is occupied by the former Jesuit College and the **Church of St Ignatius** (sv. Ignáce) 🏳. The collegiate building was constructed over a period of many years, beginning in 1659, to complement the Klementinum in the Old Town *(see page 77)*. The church itself was built between 1665–99.

From the middle of Charles Square, take Resslova Street towards the Vltava; on the right,

at the junction with Na Zderaze, is the former
★ **Church of St Carlo Borromeo** ㊵, built in the
1730s. Now known as the Church of St Cyril and
St Methodius (Kostel sv. Cyrila a Metoděje), it
serves as the cathedral of the Czech Orthodox
Church *(see also panel on facing page)*.

FAUST HOUSE

Leaving the church, head for the southern end
of Charles Square, where, at No. 40, stands the
Faust House (Faustův dům) ㊶. The history of
the house, which was given its baroque appearance in the 18th century, stretches back to the 14th
century, when it belonged to Prince Václav of
Opava, an alchemist and natural historian. In the
16th century, it was the home of Edward Kelly,
the Englishman employed by Rudolf II to search
for the Philosopher's Stone; and in the mid-18th
century, it belonged to Count Ferdinand Mladota
of Solopysky, whose chemical experiments gave
rise to its association with the Faust legend.

*St John of Nepomuk
on the Rock*

EMMAUS MONASTERY

Following the tram lines in a southerly direction
along Vyšehradská, you will come to the imposing **Church of St John of Nepomuk on the Rock**
(Kostel sv. Jana na skalce) ㊷, built in 1730 by
Kilian Ignaz Dientzenhofer. The dome fresco
(1748) by Karel Kovár depicts the church's patron
being accepted into the congregation of saints.

Opposite stands the **Emmaus Monastery**
(Klášter na Slovanech) ㊸, founded in 1347 for
Benedictine monks of the Slavic Ritual. The complex was badly damaged during an air raid on
14 February 1945. Of great artistic merit are the
Gothic frescoes, dating from about 1360, in the
cloister, some of which were destroyed. Some 80
paintings spread across the 26 wall sections portray the Life and Passion of Christ, together with
introductory scenes from the Old Testament.

The reconstruction of the exterior of the former
monastery church was completed in 1968 with
the addition of two modern towers.

Map on page 76

Below: rotunda of St Martin
Bottom: Church of SS Peter and Paul – tympanum detail

VYSEHRAD

Following the tram route southwards, the Botanical Gardens of Prague will be seen on the left. Turning into Na slupi and bearing right through the tram crossing and then left uphill via Lumirova or Přemyslova, you will eventually reach the ★★ **Vyšehrad**, the rock jutting out high above the Vltava which is regarded as the place where the city of Prague really began. It is believed that the legendary Princess Libuše, at the beginning of the 9th century, prophesied that a great city would be founded here. Between the 10th and 12th centuries, Vyšehrad was the political and religious centre of the country, then it was replaced by Hradčany, and most of its old glory paled.

Passing through the Tabor Gate (Táborská brána; 1655) and the Leopold Gate (Leopoldov brána; 1670), the visitor enters the former castle compound. On the right stands the **Rotunda of St Martin** (Rotunda sv. Martina) ⓵, dating from the end of the 11th century, and one of the three remaining Romanesque round churches in Prague.

After passing the rotunda, turn left off the main road to reach the southern part of the former fortifications, with a particularly fine view of the Vltava and the pleasure marina. Nearby is the neo-Gothic **Church of St Peter and St Paul** (sv. Petr a Pavla) ⓵, built in 1885–1903. Adjoining the church is the Memorial Cemetery and the cele-

brated Slavín Mausoleum; many famous Czechs are buried here, including the composers Bedřich Smetana (whose tombstone is in the form of an obelisk) and Antonín Dvořák (bust), as well as the writers Karel Čapek and Jan Neruda.

Vyšehrad can also be reached by underground; it is ten minutes' walk from Vyšehrad station.

Star Attraction
• Vyšehrad

CHARLES PALACE

Leave the Vyšehrad by means of Pevnostní Street, which leads through a monumental gateway, crossing back over the railway and then along Horská Street up to **Charles Palace** (Karlov) **46**. The eccentric central building, in the middle of a large courtyard, was founded in 1350 by Charles IV and dedicated by him to his personal patron and namesake, Charlemagne. The Palatinate Chapel in Aachen served as a model for the octagonal ground plan. The present vaulting was added in 1575, and during the 18th century the interior was remodelled in baroque style. The replica of the Santa Scala in Rome was also added at that time.

Pleasure cruise
Prague offers a wide array of journeys along the Vltava river, ranging from one to four hours, some offering meals and drinks. A convenient place to catch one is on the Central Wharf near to the 'Fred and Ginger' building, where several boats dock for passengers in the afternoon. One of these is the **Pražská paroplavební společnost** (tel: 224 931 013; www.paroplavba.cz); tours are also run by **EVD** (tel: 224 810 030; www.evd.cz/en/info.htm) which leave from Na františku.

DVORAK MUSEUM

Leaving the church, continue along Ke Karlovu in a northerly direction. At No. 20 is the **Villa Amerika 47**, a delightful summer palace built by Kilian Ignaz Dientzenhofer in 1717–20 for Count Michna. It acquired its present name during the 19th century when an inn of that name stood here. Today, the Villa Amerika houses the interesting **Dvořák Museum** (Muzeum A. Dvořáska; Tues–Sun 10am–5pm; www.nm.cz).

To the west, in Kateřinská Street, is the **Church of St Catherine 48**, founded by Charles IV in 1354 and rebuilt in 1737–41. The church has an elegant, octagonal steeple, but is not open to the public. From here, follow Lípová and Štěpánská back to Wenceslas Square, noticing on the right the **Church of St Stephen 49** (1351).

Opposite, in the courtyard, is the Rotunda of St Longinus, one of the city's three Romanesque round churches.

Villa Amerika

Cover map

Additional Sights

Listed below are some of the city's notable sights which lie off the routes described so far.

Below: Observation Tower on Petřín Hill
Bottom: the view of Prague

PETRIN HILL

The **Petřín Hill** lies above the Lesser Quarter. It makes a pleasant excursion and can be reached on foot from Strahov Monastery *(see page 47)*, from the Lesser Quarter Square or from Karmelitská and Újezd streets. From the latter you can also take the funicular railway. In the southwest, Petřín Hill is bordered by the Hunger Wall (Hladová zed'), erected by Charles IV in 1360–2 during a famine, when the labourers were paid in food.

On the summit of Petřín Hill stands the charming twin-towered **Church of St Lawrence** (Kostel sv Vavřinec) **50**, built between 1735–70. Somewhat further away stands the ★ **Observation Tower** **51** (daily, May–Aug 10am–10pm, Apr and Sept 10am–7pm, Oct 10am–6pm; Nov–Dec, Sat–Sun 10am–5pm), built in 1891 in imitation of the Eiffel Tower in Paris for the Jubilee Exhibition. It is 60m (197ft) high, and provides a breathtaking panorama of the city for those who are prepared to negotiate the 299 steps.

On the slopes are pretty gardens leading down towards the Lesser Quarter; these are the **Seminar**

Garden (Seminářská zahrada) **52**, the **Schönborn Garden 53** and the **Lobkowitz Garden 54**. (The latter two are not open to the public as they form part of the embassies of the USA and Germany.) To the south lies the **Kinsky Garden** (Kinského zahrada) **55** and the Kinsky Summer Palace.

It is worth descending from Petřín Hill northwards via Vlašská, passing the Welsh Hospital **56**, erected in 1602, and (at No. 19) the Lobkowitz Palace (Lobkovícký palác) **57**, built in 1703–7 and extended by the addition of another storey in 1769. Today this splendid baroque palace houses the German Embassy.

VITKOV HILL

Lying in the east of the city, **Vítkov Hill 59** can be reached from the Powder Tower via Hybernská and Husitská streets (near the main railway station). Immediately after the railway bridge, by the Museum of Military History (Armádní muzeum), turn left uphill into U památníku.

On the hill stands the National Memorial (Národní památník), a massive cube covered with granite slabs, built in 1928–38 to symbolise the struggle for independence, and containing the Tomb of the Unknown Soldier. The bronze doors depict the struggles of May 1945.

In front of the monument stands a bronze equestrian statue 9m (30ft) high, 10m (33ft) long and 5m (16ft) wide of the Hussite leader Jan Žižka, who repulsed the attacking forces of Emperor Sigismund from this spot on 14 July 1420. Created by Bohumil Kafka in 1950, it weighs 16.5 tonnes and is claimed to be the largest equestrian statue in the world.

CITY MUSEUM

To gain further insight into the history of the city, a visit to the ★**Museum of the City of Prague** (Muzeum hlavního města Prahy) **60** (Tues– Sun 9am–6pm; www.muzeumprahy.cz) is highly recommended. It is located at the end of Na poříčí (nearest underground station: Florenc). The museum's

> **Mozart's villa**
> The Villa Bertramka **58** (Mozartova 2, Smíchov; tram 4, 7, 9; underground station Anděl), will forever be linked with the name of Wolfgang Amadeus Mozart. In 1787 Mozart lived in this summer villa, the property of the Dušeks, who were both musicians. At the time, the villa lay well outside the city limits. During this period, the composer completed his opera Don Giovanni. He was to stay here again in 1789, and in 1791, when he composed his opera La Clemenzia di Tito. In 1929, the house was transformed into a museum (daily, Apr–Oct 9.30am–6pm, Nov–Mar 9.30am–4pm; www.bertramka.cz). Concerts are held here on a regular basis.

Vitkov Hill: the bronze doors

Cover map

rich collections provide a survey of the development of Prague from the earliest times until the present day. Valuable works of art and a detailed paper and wood model of the city by Antonín Langweil (1830) are among the exhibits.

Imperial Park
One of Prague's best kept secrets lies just north of the city centre, near the Výstaviště exhibition grounds. Stromovka park, formerly the Royal Hunting Grounds, is the largest green space in the city. Wandering among its rambling gardens, serene duck ponds and winding paths, you'll soon forget that you're in a city at all. A perfect setting for a sunny afternoon.

STATE OPERA

The impressive neo-Renaissance building of the ★ **State Opera** (Státní Opera) **❻** stands on Wilsonova Street between the National Museum and the main railway station. Dating from 1886–8, it has one of the loveliest auditoriums to be found anywhere in Europe. The theatre is designed in rococo style in white and gold, the hall is also renowned for its excellent acoustics. As well as innovative opera productions, ballets are also performed here.

Equestrian statue of Jan Žižka

ST AGNES CONVENT

★ **St Agnes' Convent** (Klášter sv. Anežky) **❻**, U Milosdrných Street, is situated on the northern outskirts of the Old Town, near the Vltava. The convent was founded in 1234 by Agnes, the sister of Wenceslas I; it was later extended to include a Franciscan monastery and seven churches. Closed in 1797, the convent represents the most important Early Gothic building in Prague. It rapidly fell to ruin, however, and large sections were totally destroyed. For decades restoration work has been proceeding to protect the remaining three churches and the principal convent buildings.

The convent buildings now hold the National Gallery's collection of ★★ **Medieval Art in Bohemia and Central Europe: 1200–1550** (Tues –Sun 10am–6pm; www.ngprague.cz), previously in the Monastery of St George. The superb collection has been sensitively displayed and fits well into the restored space of the convent. One of the most important exhibits is the magnificent series of six altar panels (*c.* 1380) painted by the Master of Wittingau (Třeboň) for the Augustinian monastery of Wittingau in South Bohemia. The panels – one of the summits of Bohemian painting during the 14th century – are painted on both sides: the front was displayed on holy days and the rear on normal days. The front panels depict *Christ on the Mount of Olives*, *The Burial of Christ* and *The Resurrection*; the rear portrays three saints per panel.

Other exhibits include a panel portrait of *St Elizabeth* by Master Theodoric, who painted 127 such panels for the Chapel of the Holy Cross at Karlštejn Castle *(see page 98)*, works by Lucas Cranach the Elder and Albrecht Altdorfer, as well as a number of woodcuts by Albrecht Dürer.

Star Attractions
● **Medieval Art in Bohemia and Central Europe**
● **Troja Palace**

Below: altar panel in the Medieval Art collection
Bottom: view of the city

TROJA PALACE

In the north of the city, near the zoo, is the ★★ **Troja Palace** (Trojsky Zámek: Apr–Oct, Tues–Sun 10am–6pm; Nov–Mar, Sat–Sun 10am–5pm). The huge palace complex was built in baroque style by Jean-Baptiste Mathey for Count Sternberg in 1679–85, and is famous for the staircase on the garden side, with statues representing the Titans' struggle against the gods on Mount Olympus. The palace also includes the Imperial Hall, with a large ceiling fresco (1691–7) by Abraham Godyn representing homage to the House of Habsburg, and a gallery of 19th-century Bohemian painting.

Cover map

Historic pub
If you've worked up an appetite on your journey to White Mountain, find yourself a seat in the historic Velká Hospoda (Great Tavern; Karlovarská 98, Prague 6), where you'll be treated to a fine selection of Czech specialities. Here you can reflect over a frothy mug of Czech beer in the very courtyard where monks once meditated: the pub owes its unique atmosphere to the fact that it was originally built as a chapel and monastery.

The dome of the main railway station

WHITE MOUNTAIN

The **Pilgrimage Church on the White Mountain** is situated in the west of Prague, at the terminus Bílá hora of tram No. 22 from the National Theatre. The site of the decisive victory of the Catholic army over Protestant forces in 1620 is marked by a little pilgrimage church surrounded by an ambulatory with four corner chapels, dating from the first quarter of the 18th century. The dome frescoes are the work of Cosmas Damian Asam, Johann Adam Schöpf and Wenzel Lorenz Reiner.

BENEDICTINE MONASTERY

Břevnov Monastery, in the Prague suburb of the same name, can be reached by tram No. 8 or 22. It was founded in 993 by St Adalbert as the first monastery in Bohemia, and was run by the Benedictines. Remains of a Romanesque basilica have been discovered. The present buildings (1708–40; guided tours in Czech only; Sat–Sun 10am, 2 and 4pm), were largely the work of Christoph and Kilian Ignaz Dientzenhofer.

PALACE OF ART

★ **Veletržní Palac** at Dukelskych hrdinů 47, Prague 7 (Tues–Sun 10am–6pm; www.ngprague.cz), is a mammoth space which holds the National Gallery's collection of 19th and 20th century European Art. Highlights include: *Two Women in a Garden* by Claude Monet; *The Lovers* by Auguste Renoir; *Self-Portrait* by Henri Rousseau; three paintings each by Paul Cézanne and Paul Gauguin; *The Green Cornfield* by Vincent van Gogh; *Moulin Rouge* by Toulouse-Lautrec; five still life works by Georges Braque; *The Circus* by Marc Chagall and no fewer than 14 works by Pablo Picasso.

RAILWAY STATION

Prague has many art nouveau buildings. On arrival or departure, don't ignore the main railway station (Hlavní nádraží) with its fine art nouveau sculptures and the massive glazed dome.

Excursions from Prague

With the aid of the following descriptions of sights near Prague, and the map on page 96, you should be able to draw up routes to match your own particular interests. It is also possible to join one of the day trips organised by CEDOK, or one of the other travel agents *(see page 123)*.

KARLSTEJN (KARLSTEIN)

★★ Karlštejn/Karlstein, 28km/17 miles from Prague, is the most attractive castle in Bohemia, and as such the most rewarding destination for a day trip. If travelling by car, leave Prague on the E12 in the direction of Pilsen, and take the Loděnice exit. Karlštejn can also be reached by train, from Smichovské (Metro Smíchovské nádraží). Trains depart more or less every hour and the journey takes about 25 minutes. It will take approximately 30 minutes to reach the castle from the station or slightly less from the car park.

The castle can only be viewed as part of a conducted tour, of which there are two, the first covers the Imperial Palace and the Marian Tower, the second the chapels, picture gallery and library; tour two must be booked in advance. The last tour begins one hour before the castle closes, tickets are available in the Outer Courtyard (Tues–Sun:

Map on page 96

Star Attraction
● **Karlštejn Castle**

Below: Bohemian glass
Bottom: Karlštejn Castle

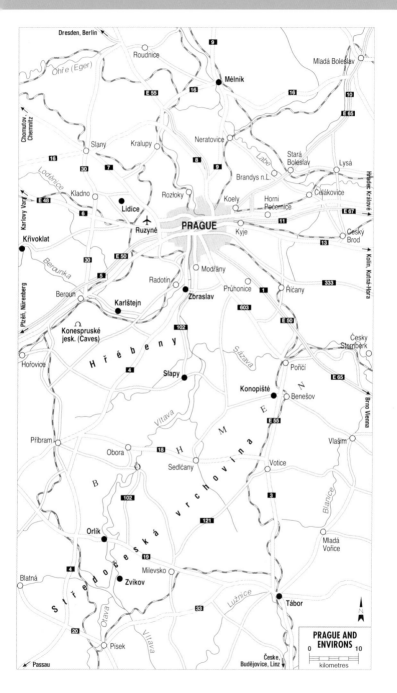

PRAGUE AND ENVIRONS

0   10

kilometres

Nov–Jan, Mar 9am–noon, 1–3pm; Apr, Oct
9am–noon, 1–4pm; May–Jun, Sept 9am–noon,
12.30–5pm; July–Aug 9am–noon, 12.30–6pm;
closed mid-Jan–Feb; www.hradkarlstejn.cz).

ARCHITECTS INVOLVED

Charles IV had the castle built in 1348–65 by two
of the most important architects of the Gothic
Age, Matthew of Arras and Peter Parler, who
were also responsible for St Vitus' Cathedral in
Prague. Here – far from the capital and impreg-
nable against outside attack – the emperor planned
to keep the Imperial Jewels, the Coronation
Insignia of the Bohemian Kings and the relics
he had gathered together from all over Europe.

Charles created the castle as a symbolic expression of his divine right to rule the Holy Roman
Empire, and the pious ruler, who was also a noted
theological scholar, planned to meditate here in
peace, surrounded by his religious treasures.
Much of building we see today is the result of a
19th-century reconstruction.

Bastion of feudal supremacy

IMPERIAL PALACE

From the Entrance **A**, the tours proceed underneath the castle to the Outer Courtyard **B**, which
also serves as an open-air theatre. Crossing the
Inner Courtyard **C** they then ascends to the
★ **Imperial Palace D**.

There are five rooms on two floors
which house a large number of exhibits.
The first floor contains some architectural
models, remains of the original stained
glass windows of the Chapel of the Holy
Cross and two wooden statues (Saints
Catherine and Nicholas) dating from the
beginning of the 15th century. On the second floor are the remains of a glass painting from the Chapel of St Catherine and
a fine diptych dating from the second half
of the 14th century. Of the private quarters of Charles IV on the second floor,
only the Audience Room has survived.

KARLSTEIN CASTLE
0   50
metres

Chapel of the Holy Cross
Newly reopened after a decades-long, painstaking restoration, Karlštejn's Chapel of the Holy Cross is the Czech Republic's answer to the Sistine Chapel, and perhaps its greatest artistic and cultural treasure. During the reign of Holy Roman Emperor Charles IV, it could even be said to have been the spiritual centre of Europe. Now, with the restoration complete, it has once again taken its place among the finest and most important medieval sanctuaries in Europe. Admission is limited. To make a reservation, book ahead by calling tel: 274 008 154.

Chapel of St Catherine

CHAPEL OF THE VIRGIN MARY

The tours continue through St Mary's Tower, where there is a **Chapel of the Virgin Mary** divided into two sections **E**, in which remains of the original frescoes (including the Horseman of the Apocalypse and a number of likenesses of Charles IV) can still be seen.

Of particular interest is the room next door, the little **Chapel of St Catherine F**. This was the emperor's private chapel, which only he was allowed to enter. He often shut himself in here for days at a time; food and documents were passed to him through a narrow opening at floor level.

The walls are decorated with approximately 1,000 semi-precious stones set in gold. On the altar, at eye level for the kneeling emperor, are portrayed Christ, the Virgin Mary and St John with companions. Above, in the altar niche, is the Virgin Mary with the Infant Jesus, to whom Charles IV and his third wife, Anna von Schweidnitz, are paying homage.

CHAPEL OF THE CROSS

A drawbridge used to lead from St Mary's Tower to the Great Tower, which contains the holy of holies, the ★★ **Chapel of the Holy Cross G**, now restored and open to the public *(see panel)*.

The chapel, completed in 1365, was planned as a single vast treasure chamber, with decorations of artistic and material value corresponding to its precious contents. The twin-trussed chapel is divided by a gilt screen. The ribbed vaulting is also covered in gold set with stars of molten glass.

The walls are set with 2,451 precious and semi-precious stones, including topazes, amethysts, jasper, onyx and chrysolite. No fewer than 1,300 golden thorns encircle the room like a ribbon, on which the candles shine. Through the quartz window, only subdued light from outside was able to penetrate. Master Theodoric, the most important Bohemian artist of the time, painted 127 exquisite portraits of saints, behind which the relics collected by the emperor were kept. He also painted the Crucifixion scene on the High Altar.

Behind the golden screen beneath were the coronation insignia and the most important relics. During the Middle Ages only the emperor, the archbishop and a few privileged people were permitted to enter, and even today the chapel has very restricted opening times.

ZBRASLAV

Zbraslav lies 10km (6 miles) south of Prague. The original Cistercian abbey was founded in 1291 and was the final resting place of the last Přemyslid rulers. The abbey was destroyed by the Hussites in 1420 and the present buildings date from 1716. Today they house the National Gallery's collection of Asian Art (Tues–Sun 10am– 6pm; www.ngprague.cz). Also worth visiting is the 17th-century baroque church.

KONOPISTE

Konopiště is 42km (26 miles) southeast of Prague, near Benešov. It can be reached by train from the Wilsonova (main) station to Benešov, then a short bus ride. This magnificent castle, dating from the 14th century, belonged to a number of aristocratic families before it was purchased in 1894 by the heir to the throne of Austria-Hungary, Archduke Francis Ferdinand, whose assassination on

Star Attraction
● **Chapel of the Holy Cross**

Below: Konopiště
garden sculpture
Bottom: Konopiště Castle

Map on page 96

28 June 1914 was the direct cause of World War I. He had it rebuilt and fitted out at enormous cost. In 82 rooms there are collections of weapons, paintings and sculptures, including many of portraits of St George, in whom the Archduke was particularly interested.

There are also a large number of valuable furnishings, dating especially from the 17th and 18th centuries and some 300,000 hunting trophies – of which, however, only 3,000 are on display.

Below: Zvíkov Castle
Bottom: Orlík Castle,
ceiling detail

CHAPEL PAINTINGS

In the bedroom of Admiral Tirpitz is a Late Gothic lindenwood sculpture, The Burial of Christ, and in the bedroom of William II there is a Florentine portrait of the Madonna, both dating from the 15th century. In the Castle Chapel, which Francis Ferdinand had restored in neo-Gothic style for the sum of 300,000 Austrian guilders, hang a number of valuable German and Italian panel paintings, wooden reliefs and winged altars. The castle park is also very attractive.

ORLIK

The history of the castle at Orlík, 80km (50 miles) south of Prague on the Vltava, reaches back into the 13th century. It was subsequently rebuilt and extended on a number of occasions. Since 1717 the castle has been in the possession of the princes of Schwarzenberg, who have embellished it with precious works of art. The castle was almost completely destroyed by fire in 1802, but it was quickly repaired and rebuilt. It has been administered by the state since 1948.

Of particular interest to visitors are the Blue Drawing Room on the first floor and the Empire-style salons on the second floor.

North of Orlík, the Vltava is dammed by a barrage. This means that the castle no longer lies as far above the water table as it once did. You can take a motor boat across the reservoir to Zvíkov (12km/7 miles). There are also facilities for bathing and water sports.

ZVIKOV

Zvíkov/Klingenberg, 92km (57 miles) from Prague, stands at the confluence of the Otava and the Vltava. The castle, erected during the 13th century by Přemysl Otakar I and King Wenceslas I, stands on a high cliff. The oldest section is the Markoman Tower, which owes its name to the fact that the Markomans originally resided here. Of particular note are the Early Gothic arcaded courtyard and the lovely frescoes.

From Zvíkov it's only 30km (19 miles) to Tábor, which has a Late Gothic Town Hall and attractive old streets.

LIDICE

Lidice, 25km (15 miles) west of Prague, lies south of the road to Slaný. This village is where the Nazis wreaked revenge for the assassination of Deputy Reichsprotektor Reinhard Heydrich. During the night of 10 June 1942, the 192 male inhabitants were shot; the women were taken to the concentration camp at Ravensbrück, where 60 of them were tortured to death. The 105 children from Lidice were taken to Lodz, from where the majority were sent to an extermination camp. The site of the former village has been turned into a poignant memorial to the victims of the massacre.

Further options…
Other possible excursion destinations from Prague include: the 13th-century royal castle of Křivoklát, 50km (31 miles) west of Prague; the stalactite caves near Koněprusy, 40km (25 miles) from Prague; the beautiful, medieval silver-mining town of ★ Kutná Hora, 64km (40 miles) east of Prague; and the wine-growing area and castle of ★ Mělnik, 30km (19 miles) north of Prague, at the confluence of the Vltava and the Elbe. Further details can be found in both the Compact Guide and the Insight Guide to the Czech Republic.

Stained glass in the church of St Barbara at Kutná Hora

Art and Architecture

Praguers like to think of their city as the 'jewel in the crown of Europe,' and, surveying the skyline from Hradčany or perched atop Petřín hill, it's difficult to argue with them. It seems a charmed city indeed; one that has survived 10 centuries of tumultuous history, 40 years of communist neglect and a decade of capitalist boom miraculously intact.

Today, Prague is a living museum of European architecture, where all phases of development are gorgeously represented – from Romanesque origins to mighty Gothic cathedrals, from splendid baroque palaces to magnificent art nouveau boulevards.

The dates quoted in brackets after the buildings listed below refer to the year in which construction began.

THE ROMANESQUE ERA

Though Prague was little more than a trading post under the Roman empire, the style left its mark on the city's sacred architecture for centuries. Hradčany contains the ruins of several early Romanesque churches, but the most obvious examples are the rotundas of St Martin, St Longinus and the Holy Cross, dating from about 1100. Prague's most important Romanesque building is St George's Basilica, which was rebuilt in 1142.

THE GOTHIC ERA

It was the advent of the Gothic in the 13th century that, more than any other architectural movement, defined the character of the city. The dozens of dramatic Gothic spires that punctuate the skyline have inspired visitors to dub Prague 'the city of 100 towers.'

The gem of Gothic Prague is without a doubt Hradčany's magnificent St. Vitus' Cathedral (1344). Its almost inconceivable complexity is the fruit of at least three architectural geniuses.

It was Matthew of Arras who began the construction of St Vitus' Cathedral (1344), as well as

Opposite: inside the Klementinum
Below and bottom: aspects of St Vitus'

Palaces and gardens
Ranking highly among the city's historical and architectural jewels are its palaces and gardens, from the Renaissance Royal Garden just to the north of the castle, containing the Belvedere Summer Palace, to the castle's South Garden with its magnificent views. Gardens belonging to the palaces of the nobility also warrant attention, most notably those of the Waldstein Palace, with their fine statuary.

The Royal Palace

Karlštejn Castle (1348), defining the future dimensions of the work. After his death the project was turned over to the young Peter Parler (1330–99), the influential master who was also responsible for Charles Bridge (1357) and the Old Town Bridge Tower (*c* 1375). And finally, the neo-Gothic builder Josef Mocker (1835–99) completed the masterpiece, incorporating elements of every Gothic style down the ages.

Examples of the high Gothic era include the Church of Our Lady of the Snows (1347), the Emmaus Monastery (1347) and the Teyn Church (1365). Later works include the Lesser Quarter Bridge Tower (1464) and the Powder Tower (1475). In about 1500, Late Gothic art in Prague reached its zenith under Benedikt Ried, who created the upper storey of the Royal Palace (including the Vladislav Hall, the Knights' Staircase and the Louis Wing) as well as the Vladislav Oratorium (1493) in St Vitus' Cathedral.

THE RENAISSANCE

Though the Renaissance was late in reaching Prague, and came to an abrupt end with the Habsburg takeover after the Battle of White Mountain in 1620, the movement left an indelible mark on the city. Architectural representatives of the era include the Belvedere Summer Palace (1534), the Schwarzenberg Palace (1543), the Star Castle (1555) and the Church of the Redeemer (1578). Emperor Rudolf II commissioned the Spanish Room and the Rudolf Gallery (1589) in Hradčany as well as the magnificent Italian Renaissance portico (1602) in the Ungelt Courtyard.

THE BAROQUE

From the stately granduer of the Troja Palace (1679) to the cherub-filled Church of St Nicholas in the Lesser Quarter (1703), lovers of the baroque in all its opulence – and gaudiness – will find much to admire in Prague.

During the first half of the 18th century, the baroque master Christoph Dientzenhofer (1655–

1722) and his son Kilian Ignaz (1689–1751) had a profound effect on the city's architecture. Dientzenhofer the Elder began the construction of the Church of St Nicholas in the Lesser Quarter, the Břevnov Monastery (1708) and the Loreto Shrine (1717); his son continued the work.

The latter was also responsible for the Villa Amerika (1717), the Church of St John of Nepomuk on the Rock (1730) and the Church of St Nicholas in the Old Town (1732).

Below: Koruna Palace detail, Wenceslas Square
Bottom: Typical Prague quirkiness – Frank Gehry's 'Ginger and Fred' Building

ART NOUVEAU

Though the movement was founded in France at the beginning of the 20th century, Prague soon outstripped Paris as the best home of art nouveau architecture. Indeed, the playful spirit and delicate ornamentation of the style seem to fit the city like a designer glove.

The most splendid example is the Municipal House on Wenceslas Square, by Osvald Polívka and Antonín Balšánek, and the magnificent façades of Pařížká street form a remarkable urban ensemble of classic art nouveau style. But the name synonymous with art nouveau in Prague is Alfonse Mucha (1860–1939), the Czech artist who gained fame for his posters of the actress Sarah Bernhardt. His delightful prints can be found in souvenir shops throughout the city.

Literature

More than any other writer, Franz Kafka *is* Prague. Born in 1883, Kafka almost never left the city centre until shortly before his death in 1924 – he aptly dubbed Prague 'the little mother with claws.' His masterpiece, *The Castle,* leaves no doubt about the city's influence on his work, from the Old Town's labyrinthine streets to Hradčany's brooding presence.

Kafka was born in the house called The Tower, on the square that now bears his name just off the Old Town Square. He lived with his parents for most of his life at various addresses in the city, including the cottage of his favourite sister, Ottla, in The Golden Lane *(see page 36)*. He also rented a two-room flat in the Schönborn Palace, which today is the US Embassy. After his death in 1924, Kafka was buried in the New Jewish Cemetery (Nový Židovský hřbitov), near the metro station Zelivskeho. Kafka's best work, such as *Metamorphosis*, depicts the confusion and alienation of individuals faced with bureaucratic authority.

Rehabilitating Kafka

Like many of Prague's great figures, Franz Kafka spoke German – an unfortunate fact that caused his work to go out of favour after the Czechs were finally rid of the Austro-Hungarian empire in 1918, and with the expulsion of ethnic Germans in 1945. The communists, too, rejected Kafka as a bourgeois intellectual. But now, there are signs that Kafka is being embraced by Czechs at last. The square where he was born was renamed after him in 2000, and a recent exhibition of 'Great Czech Writers' began with Kafka.

Kafka rehabilitated

GERMAN-SPEAKING WRITERS

Egon Erwin Kisch (1885–1948), the 'roving reporter' who did much to influence the style and substance of journalism as we know it today, was

born and lived for many years in the house called 'The Two Bears' *(see page 63)*, now a museum.

The poet Rainer Maria Rilke (1875–1926) was born at Jindřišská ulice 19, opposite the main post office. At the age of 11 he was sent to the military secondary school at St Pölten. Between 1892–6, he attended grammar school in Prague once more. In 1896, his first works, the *Larenopfer*, an anthology of poems about Prague and other Bohemian subjects, were published there. After 1896, he returned to Prague only for brief visits.

Of the many other German-speaking writers whose names are closely linked with the city, it will suffice to mention Gustav Meyrink (1868–1932), the editor of the book *The Golem*, and Max Brod (1884–1968), Kafka's friend and literary executor.

CZECH WRITERS

Virtually all important Czech writers of the late 19th and early 20th centuries lived in Prague for a considerable part of their lives. They include the Romantic lyric poet Karel Hynek Mácha (1810–36), whose epic poem *May* (1836) is regarded as one of the milestones in modern Czech poetry; the collector of Czech folk songs and fairy tales, Karel Jaromir Erben (1811–70); and Božena Němcová (1820–62), the author of the novel *Grandmother*. There are three others who have achieved greater fame beyond the boundaries of their native country.

Jan Neruda (1834–91) compiled the *Tales of the Lesser Quarter*, a collection of novellas and partly humourous, partly reflective sketches from the Malá Strana. He lived for many years in the house called 'The Two Suns' *(see page 53)*, in the street now named Nerudova in his honour. He was a disciple of Romanticism but developed into the foremost classical poet in modern Czech literature.

Jaroslav Hašek (1882–1923), a compulsive and accomplished practical joker and committed anarchist, achieved world fame as the author of *The Good Soldier Švejk*, a brilliantly incisive satire on military life, and still the best-known book in the Czech language. Švejk, an irresponsible and

Below: Kisch Memorial
Bottom: Kafka in bronze

I, Robot

There is only one word in the English language that comes from Czech: 'robot', coined by the novelist and playwright Karel Čapek (1890–1938), who lived and died at Ulice Bratří Čapků in the Vinohrady district. Much of his work deals with the problems of a centrally organised machine age, and 'RUR' – in which 'robot' appears – describes the construction of a man-like machine which, ironically, is in every way better than its creator.

undisciplined drunkard, liar and scrounger, is widely thought to be at least partly autobiographical in inspiration. Having deserted the Austrian army in 1915, he crossed over to the Russian side, but managed to make satirical attacks on both régimes. His favourite pub, U kalicha (The Chalice), is a great tourist attraction today.

More recent Czech-born writers include Jaroslav Seifert, who was awarded the Nobel prize for literature in 1984; Milan Kundera, whose work includes *The Unbearable Lightness of Being* (1984); Ivan Klíma, born in 1931; and, of course, the president, Václav Havel.

Music

The documentory evidence for the musical traditions of Bohemia stretches right back to the Early Middle Ages, but it wasn't until the 19th century, after the reawakening of the Czech national consciousness, that Czech composers and their music were able to assert themselves at home. Until then, many musicians had little alternative but to emigrate, to cities like Vienna, Paris and Rome, while their place was taken in Prague by a long line of illustrious visitors.

Josef Lada's image of the Good Soldier Švejk

MOZART'S PRAGUE

Wolfgang Amadeus Mozart (1756–91) came to Prague for the first time in January of 1787, and instantly fell in love with the city, where he said he enjoyed greater freedom and inspiration than in overbearing Vienna. He returned to Prague in August the same year, and stayed initially in the inn, The Three Golden Lions, on the Coal Market, where a commemorative plaque recalls his visit. He then moved into the Bertramka summer villa (today a museum, *see page 91*), the property of a musician named Dušek and his wife. There he completed *Don Giovanni*, inspired by the real-life Casanova, whom Mozart befriended in Prague. He conducted the premiere himself at the Nostitz Theatre (now the Estates Theatre) on 29 October 1787. It was a roaring success.

He spent 1789 travelling backwards and forwards from Berlin, staying at Bertramka for a short period each time. It was here, in 1791, that he composed *La Clemenzia di Tito* in only 18 days; the opera also had its premiere in the Nostitz Theatre, on 6 September 1791. Three months later, Mozart died in poverty and almost forgotten in Vienna. In Prague, however, a requiem composed for the occasion was performed before a large congregation of mourners in the Church of St Nicholas in the Lesser Quarter.

Below: Smetana's grave
Bottom: a Prague concert

THE CZECH MUSIC GREATS

Bedřich Smetana (1824–84) spent most of his life in Prague. He lived at Železná ulice 548, on the corner of the Old Town Square (commemorative plaque). One of his biggest preoccupations was the creation of the first Czech popular opera, and in 1868 he conducted the premiere of the fruit of his labours, *Libuše*, as the first performance in the newly completed National Theatre.

He gave the world the most frequently performed Czech opera, *The Bartered Bride*, and he celebrated the countryside and history of his native land in the music cycle *My Fatherland*, whose most famous movement, *The Moldau*, continues to transfix the listener with its powerful emotions. His grave is in the cemetery on the

Vyšehrad *(see page 89)*, and a Smetana Museum *(see page 79)* has been set up in a house by the Vltava, near the Charles Bridge.

Antonín Dvořák (1841–1904) was the master of the symphony, chamber music and oratorio. Unlike Smetana, he attracted fame abroad during his own lifetime. His first triumph was in London, where his *Stabat Mater* was rapturously received, followed by New York, Berlin, Vienna and Budapest. In 1891 Dvořák went to America as the director of the New York Conservatory, and it was here that he produced his most popular orchestral score, Symphony No. 9 *From the New World*.

Dvořák left an impressive collection of compositions: 31 works of chamber music, 14 string quartets, 50 orchestral works and nine symphonies, such as the catchy melodies enshrined in his *Slavonic Dances*. Apart from his time in America, Dvořák lived most of his life in Prague, and his grave is also on the Vyšehrad. There is a Dvořák Museum in the Villa Amerika *(see page 89)*.

No description of Czech music is complete without a mention of the great composer Leos Janacek (1854–1928). His music drew greatly on Czech folk music and the rhythms of the Czech language.

Below: Antonín Dvořák
Bottom: detail of the Villa Amerika, home of the Dvořák Museum

CONCERTS AND FESTIVALS

Prague boasts three symphony orchestras as well as a number of chamber orchestras. The most famous concert hall is the Rudolfinum's Dvořák Hall on Náměstí Jan Palacha. You can also enjoy concerts in many of the city's churches and palaces.

The concert season proper begins in mid-September, when the Czech Philharmonic and the Prague Symphony Orchestra begin their cycle of concerts, which run throughout the winter *(see* www.czechphilharmonic.cz and www.fok.cz).

Theatre *(Divadlo)*

Paris has one theatre for every 90,000 inhabitants, and Berlin one for every 150,000. Prague, on the other hand, has a theatre for every 40,000 citizens; no wonder that Czechs elected a playwright –

Václav Havel – as their president. There are three state-run theatres: the **National Theatre**, tel: 224 901 668 (www.nationaltheatre.cz); the **Estates Theatre**, tel: 224 227 266 (www.estatestheatre.cz); and the **State Opera**, tel: 224 227 266 (www.opera.cz).

Among the best of the independent theatres are: **Theatre on the Balustrades** (www.nazabradli.cz), Anenské náměstí 5, where Havel's plays were first performed, tel: 222 868 868; **Archa Theatre** (www.archatheatre.cz), Na Poříčí 26, Prague 1, tel: 221 716 111, avant-garde theatre, dance and music with visiting foreign performers; **Divadlo Ta Fantastika** (www.tafantastika.cz), Karlova 8, tel: 222 221 366, black-light theatre, one of the best; **Laterna Magica** (www.laterna.cz), Národní třída 4, tel: 224 931 482. This last theatre, with its inimitable mixture of drama, film and ballet and unusual optical and acoustic effects, is the most famous in Prague. The actors appear to step from the stage directly into film, and vice-versa; the 'polyecran technique' can be projected onto eight screens simultaneously.

Prague Spring

The most important event in the musical calendar is undoubtedly the Prague Spring International Music Festival, held each year from mid-May until early June (www.festival.cz). The traditional festival opener – a performance of Smetana's 'My Fatherland' in the elaborate art nouveau Municipal House – is the see-and-be-seen event of the year. As a counterpart to the Prague Spring, the Prague Autumn festival has also been instituted (Oct–Nov; www.pragueautumn.cz).

PUPPET THEATRES

Prague is home to a long tradition of puppet theatre, and venues include Divadlo na Královské cestě, Karlova 12, tel: 222 220 928; and the National Marionette Theatre (Národní divadlo marionet), Žatecká 1, tel: 224 819 322.

Marionette Theatre

FOOD AND DRINK

The menu in typical Prague restaurants may not be as varied as in other cities, but the food on offer is tasty and satisfying – albeit sometimes on the heavy side. Most local dishes contain a large proportion of meat.

SPECIALITIES

The most famous culinary speciality in Prague, indeed in Bohemia as a whole, is the dumpling *(knedlíky)*, eaten above all with roast pork *(vepřová pečeně)*, the favourite local dish, and served mostly with sauerkraut *(kyselé zelí)*.

Popular hors d'oeuvres include sardines *(sardinky)*, pâté *(paštika)*, garnished herring *(sled's přilohou)*, cold meat *(studené maso)* and tongue in aspic *(jazyk v rosolu)*.

Soups of many kinds are served and some are almost a meal in themselves. The most popular soup *(polévky)* is undoubtedly the Bohemian potato soup *(bramboračka* or *bramborová polévka)*, whose principal ingredients are boiled potatoes and mushrooms. Another favourite is beef soup *(hovězí polévka)*.

As far as fish dishes *(masité pokrmy)* are concerned, carp *(kapr)* cooked in a variety of ways is the most popular; it is eaten in virtually every household at Christmas. Trout *(pstruh)* is also frequently available.

Favourite meat dishes, apart from roast pork, are beef *(hovězí maso)*, loin of beef/fillet of beef *(svíčová pečeně)*, braised beef *(dušená svíčková)*, goulash *(guláš)*, steak *(biftek)*, tongue *(jazyk)*, escalope of veal *(vídeňský řízek)*, roast veal *(telecí pečeně)*, beef olives *(ruláda)*, smoked meat *(uzené maso)*, smoked sausage *(uzenka)* and the famous Prague ham *(pražská šunka)*. Hot frankfurter-type sausages *(párky)* and fried sausages *(klobása)* are sold on the streets until late at night. Game and poultry are also popular, especially goose *(husa)* and roast duck *(kachna na roštu)*, mostly served with dumplings and sauerkraut.

A great local speciality in Prague are the many desserts. Here, too, dumplings are the main favourites, filled with plums *(švestky)*, sweet cherries *(třešně)*, morello cherries *(višně)* or apricots *(meruňky)*. Another popular dessert is pancakes *(palačinka)*. There are also a variety of local cakes, many of which, however, are very sweet.

DRINKS

Czech beer *(pivo)* is probably the finest in the world. Its quality is largely thanks to the famous hops, which have been cultivated in Northern Bohemia ever since the Middle Ages. The principal hop centre is Žatec (Saaz). In Prague, both light *(světlé)* as well as dark *(tmavé* or *černé)* beer is available.

The most famous beers are *Pilsener Urquell* from Plzeň (Pilsen), *Budvar* from České Budějovice (Budweis) and *Zlatý Bazant* (Golden Pheasant), the renowned Slovak beer. The beer from Prague's Smíchov brewery is also very good, and then there is the strong dark beer brewed on the premises at U Fleků. Another strong beer is Bránické from the Prague district of Braník.

Favourite tipples
A popular beverage – a kind of national drink – is the powerful plum schnapps *(sliwowitz/slivovice)*. The bitters from Carlsbad, known as *Becherovka*, are also enjoyed all over the country.

The wine bars, known as *vinárna*, serve predominantly Czech wines. Very good wine *(víno)* comes from Žernoseky in the Elbe Valley, where the Mělník wines are also cultivated. Excellent wines are also produced in Southern Moravia, in places like Mikulov, Hodonín, Znojmo or Valtice. Red is *červené,* white is *bílé.*

NIGHTLIFE

Prague has a lively, if techno dominated, club and jazz scene. Here are some of the best popular venues:

AghaRTA, Krakovská 5, tel: 222 211 275. Usually the best live jazz in town, often with visitng foreign artists.

Radost FX, Bělehradská 120, tel: 603 181 500. Despite being around since 1993, Radost is still a top dance club.

Reduta, Národni třída 16, tel: 224 933 487. A popular jazz venue featuring top local and visiting artists.

Roxy, Dlouhá 33, tel: 224 826 296. Popular club with an assortment of music and guest DJs. Couscous café and tearoom on premises.

U staré paní, Michalská 9, tel: 603 551 680; www.jazzinprague.com. Expensive jazz club/restaurant/hotel with excellent local and foreign bands.

History and detail at a Lesser Quarter restaurant

Eating and Drinking

These suggestions for places to eat and drink are listed alphabetically by area, and priced according to the following categories: **€€€** = expensive; **€€** = moderate; **€** = inexpensive.

Hradčany and Malá Strana

David, Tržiště 21, tel: 257 533 109. Tucked away down a quiet, atmospheric backstreet, this is a lovely place. Discrete but friendly service, and stylishly-executed Czech and modern European dishes, all backed up by an excellent selection of Moravian and French wines. **€€€**

Hergetova Cihelná, Cihelná 2b, tel: 257 535 534. Part of the Kampa Park empire, with a similarly good view of the Charles Bridge. The food is predominantly Italian (good pizza and pasta) with a few modern Czech dishes (potato soup). The desserts include delicious vodka-marinated raspberries. The service is excellent and the surroundings modern and clean. **€€**

Kampa Park, Na kampě 8b, tel: 296 826 102. One of the best places to eat in Malá Strana, and the view – of the Charles Bridge – is certainly spectacular. The restaurant has restrained and tasteful decor, and a predominance of fish on the menu. Whether it quite

lives up to the hype is debatable, but try the excellent value set lunch for a taste of the well-regarded food. €€€
Malý Buddha, Úvoz 44, tel: 220 513 894. A serene tea-house atmosphere is the setting for fresh and delicious Asian cuisine, such as spring rolls and glass noodles with vegetables, along with an impressive selection of exotic juices. €
Pálffy Palác, Valdštejnská 14, tel: 257 530 522. Go through the door in the right hand side of the imposing gateway and all the way up the stairs. The dining hall exudes a faded opulence, and a gilded chandelier and palms set off the yellowing walls. The food is competent, nothing special, a combination of French and Czech. What counts are the surroundings. €€–€€€
Restaurant Gitanes, Tržiště 7, tel: 257 530 163. A quirky and comfortable Bosnian/Serbian/Montenegran restaurant with a prettily-painted floral ceiling and furnishings, plus a cosy hideaway for two behind a curtain. The good Balkan dishes (stuffed peppers, homemade lamb sausage, grilled mushrooms) and an eclectic and interesting winelist mean this is well worth a visit. €€
Square, Malostranské nám. 5, tel: 257 532 109. A famous café given a makeover. The modern interior is stylish and well thought out. A good place for breakfast before heading up the hill to the castle, or for a light lunch or dinner from the bistro-style menu. €€
St Nicholas Café, Tržiště 10, tel: 257 530 204. A subterranean coffee house/bar with a vaulted ceiling, popular with younger locals and expats. Apart from good *Urquell* pilsner, there is a long and tempting cocktail list. €
U Patrona, Dražického nám. 4, tel: 257 530 725. These elegant little dining rooms are a good place to try well prepared Bohemian specialities. They include a tasty game consomé and

> **U Černého Vola**
> This traditional pub (Loretánské náměstí 1, tel: 220 513 481, tucked away near the Loreto Church, is one of the best-loved in the city. Decorated with coats-of-arms on white walls, it consists of a couple of rooms filled with long, wooden benches and tables, usually packed with locals. The cheap and extremely tasty Velkopopovický Kozel beer (both dark and light) keeps coming and slips down almost too easily. Food here doesn't extend much beyond sausages, bread and mustard, but it goes well with the unpretentious air of the place and, of course, the beer. €

excellent roast goose with red cabbage. All helped along by some very smooth service. €€€
U Zeleného Čaje, Nerudova 19, tel: 257 530 027. While pretty much everywhere on Nerudova is best avoided as a tourist trap, this is an honorable exception. A quiet tea house with a large range of teas and excellent strudel; it hasn't even suffered from starring in *Amadeus*. €

Staré Město and Nové Město
Ariana, Rámová 6, tel: 222 323 438. The only Afghan restaurant in Prague, this surprisingly affordable little gem offers seared chicken and turkey kebabs set on giant mounds of fluffy basmati rice. The staff make their own *dogh* (Persian yoghurt drink). €€
Arzenal, Valentinská 11, tel: 224 814 099. Part gallery, part restaurant, this Thai gem was designed by the same person responsible for the Kyoto Opera in Japan and Karl Lagerfeld's Paris store. An authentic menu features amazing pad Thai and other specialties. €€–€€€
Barock, Pařížká 24, tel: 222 329 221. Like its partner Pravda opposite, this is a place for posing. Well made espressos and calorie-laden breakfasts

are replaced by international dishes at lunch, before the space turns into more of a bar later in the evening. Large pictures of minimally-dressed models provide the decor. €€

Café and Galerie Louvre, Národní třída 20, tel: 224 930 949. This elegant art nouveau cafe with newspapers from around the world still echoes with the ghosts of noted Czech intellectuals. Choose from a long list of surprisingly affordable dishes, or go for a basic breakfast of jam, butter, honey and a basket of rolls. €

Chez Marcel, Haštalská 12, tel: 222 315 676. The bustling, informal charm of a French brasserie has been transplanted onto this quiet side street in the Old Town. Delicious fresh salads, good steaks and hand-cut chips; daily specials such as moules frites or ratatouille. The crème brûlée is consistently flawless. €

Cicala, Žitna 43, tel: 222 210 375. Despite its indistinct appearance and location on a street roaring with commuter traffic, this restaurant has thrived on awesome word of mouth, and for good reason. The owner treats every guest like a celebrity (and there are plenty of real ones too – just look at the pictures on the walls), while the kitchen staff dishes up what may be the most authentic Italian food in the entire city. €€€

Country Life, Melantrichova 15, tel: 224 213 366. Tasty all-vegetarian or vegan food, served cafe-style. The salad bar is extraordinarily bountiful by any standard. Local vegetarians swear by the soups and pizzas. €

Don Giovanni, Karolíny světlé 34, tel: 222 222 060. A long-standing Italian restuarant with very tasty and surprisingly authentic food. Comfortable with good service, dishes range from straightforward pasta to expensive seafood. There is also a good range of Italian wines. €€€

Ebel Coffee House, Týn 2, tel: 224 895 788. some of the best coffee in Prague, served any way you like, with a mind boggling selection of roasts. All of these can be bought, along with a wide variety of teas, at the nearby Vzpomínky na Afriku (on Rybná/ROH Jakubské). €

Francouzská Restaurace v Obecním domě, Náměstí republiky 5, tel: 222 002 770. An opulent hall of soaring Art Deco fixtures, smoky glass and giant windows, this gem offers sumptuous French dishes at reasonable prices. Lunch specials include appetisers and entrees like duck paté with cumberland sauce. For cheaper food in the same surroundings try the café across the entrance hall, or the Czech restaurant in the basement. €€€

Kavárna Slavia, Národní třída at Smetanovo nábřeži, tel: 224 239 604. Prague's most important cafe, with Art Deco decor, affords lovely views onto National Avenue and Prague Castle. Composer Bedřich Smetana and poet Jaroslav Seifert were former denizens. Nowadays the cafe caters to both Czechs and tourists. Service can be casual and the coffees and light meals are unremarkable, but it has a beautiful setting. €

Pub etiquette

Beer halls are an institution in Bohemia, and over the centuries a few unwritten rules have evolved. If a man and a woman enter a pub together, the man always leads in case there's trouble inside. Never bother the waiter, and always ask for his assistance before moving chairs. Place a beer coaster on the table to signal that you want a beer. Don't tip too much (a few crowns will do), otherwise you'll be perceived as arrogant. Always toast your neighbours before drinking, looking them in the eye. And never complain about a large head on a beer – that's just the way it's done.

King Solomon, Široká 8, tel: 224 818 752. This is the only strictly kosher restaurant in Prague; however, it is pricey. The surroundings are undoubtedly pleasant but the food is a bit uninspiring. There are all the expected dishes, gefilte (cold, stuffed) fish and borscht, and a range of kosher wines. If you are concerned to eat an orthodox diet it is possible to arrange Shabat meals beforehand and have them delivered to your hotel. €€€

Klub Architektů, Betlémské náměstí 169/5a, tel: 224 401 214. Just opposite the Bethlehem Church and under an architecture bookshop. As well as a few meaty things, there are lots of vegetarian offerings, salads, soups and more exotic dishes, served up in a minimalist, bare-walled cellar (appropriate given the architects above and the Hussite church close by). Friendly staff and low prices add to its attractions, as does the no-smoking area. €

La Perle de Prague, Rašínovo nábřeží 80, tel: 221 984 160. Tasteful French restaurant crowning the dancing "Fred and Ginger" building with a jaw-dropping view of the Vltava. A seasonal menu features showcase dishes such as herb-crusted rack of lamb and duck breast carpaccio in nut oil. Balcony seating during the summer. €€€

Pivovarský dům, Lípová 15, tel: 296 216 666. This microbrewery, with its traditional Czech decor and pub-like atmosphere, features an expansive menu of tough-to-find Czech specialities including fruit-filled dumplings covered in a soft, creamy cheese. The beer list boasts some fairly unorthodox flavours, such as coffee and champagne. €€

Pravda, Pařížká 17, tel: 222 326 203. A self-conciously cool restaurant that isn't shy of telling you which famous faces have been seen here. The 'global' cuisine is presented in large portions with a, sometimes, slightly fanciful nationality attached to it on the menu, and the staff are friendly and attentive. There are good-looking fish dishes and tasty vegetarian options. €€€

Tretter's, V kolkovně 3, tel: 224 811 165. A classy cocktail bar with a 1930s feel. The wonderful drinks – perhaps the best in Prague – are prepared from an interesting and comprehensive list. €€

U Fleků, Křemencova 11, tel: 224 934 019. The malthouse and brewery both date from 1459. Perhaps the most famous beer hall in Prague, U Fleků is often filled with table-pounding tourists singing along to accordion players (and sometimes even without the accordion). The beer's a little pricey, but excellent. €€

U Medvídků, Na perštýně 7, tel: 224 211 916. The 'Little Bears' is a traditional restaurant and pub (and former brewery) dishing up hearty South Bohemian and Old Czech food, accompanied by tasty Budvar beer. €

V Zátiší, Liliová 1, tel: 222 221 155. A warm, if slightly kitsch atmosphere. Highly recommended, the food mostly consists of Czech/modern European meat dishes. The desserts are excellent and range from rhubarb and apple pie, to cardamon creme brulée with poached plums.There are also *degustation* portions, so you can try a number of dishes. €€€

Zahrada v Opeře, Legerova 75, tel: 224 239 685. The outside of this restaurant initially looks a bit threatening, given the armed guards (there to protect Radio Free Europe in the same building). However, this is a treat that should not be missed. The chic interior and ultra-smooth service soon put you at ease. The food is excellent: tasty soups, garlicky grilled calamari, and some of the best desserts in Prague. €€–€€€

SHOPPING

The city offers something for just about everybody. Whether it's designer fashion or traditional handmade souvenirs you're after, you'll find it here – often at prices considerably lower than in the West. There are the Czech established department stores such as **Kotva** on Náměstí republiky, **Krone** on Václavské náměstí and **Bílá Labut** in Na poříčí. These have been joined by foreign big-name stores such as **Tesco** on Národní třída. The main shopping district is in the streets around Wenceslas Square. The street at the foot of the square, Na příkopě, is packed with shops. Pařížská is the location of most international fashion outlets.

TRADITIONAL SOUVENIRS

The city's traditional souvenirs are favourites among visitors. Bohemian glassmaking has a centuries-long tradition, and rivals Venice for the quality of its crystal. Wooden toys have always been a popular gift item as well. Delicious Prague ham is sold in butcher's shops, and the herbal liqueur Becherovka from Carlsbad makes a

Bohemian glass on sale in the Old Town Square

nice gift. The antique shops scattered throughout the city, known as *antikvariáts*, also hold hidden treasures.

Books
Anagram Books, Týn 4, Staré Město, www.anagram.cz. **Big Ben Bookshop**, Malá štupartská 5, Staré Město, www.bigbenbookshop.com. **The Globe Bookstore and Coffeehouse**, Pštrossova 6, Nové Město, www.globebookstore.cz

Glass
Moser, Na příkopě 12, Nové Město, www.moser-glass.com. **Erpet**, Staroměstské nám 27, Staré Město, www.erpet.cz

Wooden toys and crafts
Manufaktura, Melantrichova 17, Staré Město, www.manufaktura.biz. A chain of stores across the city centre.

Music
Bontonland (formerly Supraphon), Jungmannova 20, Nové Město. **Bontonland Megastore**, Václavské náměstí 1, Nové Město.

Czech Modernist Replicas
Kubista, Dům u Černé Matky Boží, Celetná 34/Ovocný trh, www.kubista.cz

PRACTICAL INFORMATION

Getting There

BY AIR

Prague is firmly on the international air grid, and is directly linked to virtually every European capital, including London, from where the flight time is only 1½ hours. The national carrier is ČSA (Czech Airlines, www.czechairlines.com). Many airlines fly from New York to Prague, and in the case of the ČSA the flight is non-stop. Low cost airlines Smart Wings (www.smartwings.net) and easyJet (www.easyjet.com) have flights to Prague. Check also with travel agents.

Prague Ruzyně airport lies 20km (13 miles) northwest of the city. There are public bus services to the centre, as well as taxis and hire cars. The company Cedaz (tel: 220 114 296) runs a shuttle bus service between the airport and Náměstí republiky, half-hourly between 5.30am and 9.30pm. The journey takes approximately 30 minutes and costs a nominal sum. For an extra fee they will drop you at your hotel. Alternatively, the number 119 bus runs to the metro stop at Dejvická, from where it is easy to get into town. Bus 100 runs to the Zličín, but this is less convenient for most vistors.

BY RAIL

There is no through service to Prague from London or Paris. For visitors travelling by train from the UK, Eurostar runs between London (Waterloo) and either Brussels or Paris (Gare du Nord). The onward service is long and frustating, either via Frankfurt, Zürich or Berlin from Paris, or Nürnberg from Brussels (tel: 08708 371 371, or *see* www.raileurope.co.uk).

There are direct train connections to Prague from Germany and Austria. All trains from southern Germany and Austria come in at the main Wilsonova Station (Hlavní nádraží). Trains from Berlin come into Prague-Holešovice Station.

BY COACH

Eurolines (www.eurolines.co.uk) operates buses that connect the major cities of Europe. It is better value than the train.

BY CAR

Although easily reached by car from Western Europe, there is no point in having your car once you are in Prague. For those who must travel this way, the main border crossings are as follows: **Nürnberg** via Waidhaus/Rozvadov (171km/106 miles); **Munich** via Bayrisch Eisenstein/Železná Rudá (171km/106 miles); **Berlin** via Zinnwald/Cínovecb (90km/56 miles); **Salzburg** via Linz Summerau/Horni Dvořistě (186 km/115 miles); **Vienna** via Gmünd/České Velenice (195km/121 miles) or Grametten/Nová Bystřice (177km/110 miles).

Drivers must be over the age of 21, and require vehicle registration papers, a valid driving licence and a nationality sticker. The maximum speed limit on country roads is 90kph/56mph, on motorways and major trunk roads it is 110kph/68mph, and in built-up areas 60kph/37mph.

In case of breakdown...
It is often difficult to obtain the necessary spare parts for foreign vehicles. The agency Yellow Angels, a non-stop emergency service for tourists and motorised visitors, can be reached by calling 123, 154 or 1240. They normally have on hand people who speak English or German, or who at least can give you directions to the next garage.

👁 Parking

Hradčany, Wenceslas Square and the surrounding streets, as well as large sections of the Old Town, are closed to motor traffic (except for access for hotel guests). In the city centre only cars with official permits may be parked. Public car parks (fee-paying) can be found near the National Theatre, the main railway station, beside the Vltava in the vicinity of the Hotel Intercontinental, between Masaryk Station and the Vltava promenade, and near the larger hotels. Illegally parked vehicles are frequently towed away or clamped; information can be obtained at the nearest police station.

Getting Around

PUBLIC TRANSPORT

The various means of public transport are cheap and well synchronised. The network includes trams and buses, the Metro and the funicular up the Petřín Hill. Tickets can be purchased in shops, at the kiosks of the Prague Public Transport Executive and from the automatic ticket machines at the stops or stations. A non-transfer ticket of 8 Kč is valid on trams or buses for 15 minutes, or 4 stops on the Metro; a 12 Kč ticket allows travel (with changes) for 60 minutes between 5am–8pm Mon–Fri, and for 90 minutes after 8pm or weekends. These must be stamped inside the trams and buses and before entering the Metro, where the yellow stamping machines are located directly at the entrance. There are no ticket or stamping machines on the platforms, so make sure that you buy a ticket at the entrance and have it stamped before you go through.

There are also special tourist tickets which allows an unlimited number of journeys within a fixed period of 1–15 days. The more expensive **Prague Card** (www.praguecard.info) gives you unlimited use of public transport for 72 hours, as well as free entrance to over 40 different sites, including the Castle, National Gallery and several museums.

Transport on the entire network is completely free for Czech children under six and Czech adults over 70. Children under 16 only pay half fare. For ticket sales and further information, contact the information line, tel: 296 191 817 (daily 7am–9pm) or check on the the the transport executive's website (www.dp-praha.cz).

THE PRAGUE METRO

The modern underground system links the centre with the suburbs and provides for convenient changes inside the city. It is a remarkably clean and quick means of public transport. The three lines have been developed with an eye towards expediency, and by changing lines it is possible to reach just about all the important tourist attractions located within the city.

The lines intersect at three main stations. From Můstek station at the bottom of Wenceslas Square you can take the green Line A over to the Lesser Quarter and Hradčany. The yellow Line B runs south to Charles Square and to the Smíchovské nádraži station. The Florenc bus station and the northeast can be reached by travelling in the opposite direction. Line A intersects with the red Line C at the Muzeum station, at the upper end of Wenceslas Square. The latter runs north to the main station, then to the Florenc bus station, where it intersects with Line B before continuing to the terminus Nádraží Holešovice, the railway station for the majority of the trains on the Berlin to Budapest route. To the south it leads down to Vyšehrad. Because of the frequency of the trains (every 5–12 minutes), you need plan for little more than 30 minutes even for journeys out into the suburbs. The Metro operates 5am–midnight.

The green 'M' signs outside the stations are small and decidedly inconspicuous. But inside, the stations, often beautifully designed, are clean and clearly laid out. Network plans are prominently located at all entrances and above the platforms; the station you are at is highlighted; the stations you can change at are marked with the colour of the intersecting line.

TRAMS AND BUSES

Prague has a comprehensive bus route network: buses *(autobus)* and trolley buses *(tramvaje)* run all day, and are particularly frequent in the suburbs, to connect with the Metro.

Among the many tram and bus routes within Prague, Line 22 is probably the most interesting for visitors. It runs from Náměstí míru over Charles Square and along the Národní třída (National Street). It crosses the Vltava and then runs along the Karmelitská in the Lesser Quarter to the Lesser Quarter Square. From there it winds its way up Castle Hill, and on along the Keplerova to the starting point for Strahov and Petřín Hill. On Line 22 it is possible to have an almost complete tour of the city for only a few crowns. This is an ideal way of making a first acquaintance with many of the sights.

SIGHTSEEING AND EXCURSIONS

During the summer months, the tram offers the possibility of a sightseeing

tour of the city along two different routes (lines 91 and 92). You can board, for example, by the main railway station, the National Theatre, or on the Malostranská náměstí.

A number of travel agents, including CEDOK, organise sightseeing tours by coach. Departures are from the coach park at Bílkova 6 (opposite the Hotel Intercontinental).

Apart from these regular tours, there are also special tours organised around a central theme, including 'Romanesque Prague', 'Gothic Prague', 'The Prague of the Renaissance', 'The Prague of the Baroque Era', 'Musical Prague', etc. Popular one-day excursions to destinations outside the city include 'The Castles and Palaces of Bohemia', 'Castles and Palaces along the Vltava', 'Pearls of Bohemian Gothic' and 'To the beauty spots of Southern Bohemia'.

One of the best vantage points for viewing Prague is, of course, the river Vltava. For further information on river cruises, *see page 89.*

Facts for the Visitor

PASSPORTS AND VISAS
For citizens of most European countries as well as the United States and Canada, no visa is required. Nationals of other countries are advised to contact their respective Czech embassies or consulates for information.

Rider beware
Prague's taxi drivers have earned a bad reputation for overcharging foreign visitors to the city. It's best to avoid standing taxis and hail a moving one instead, especially near major tourist sites. Fares are regulated, so always make sure the driver turns on the meter. The initial charge is 34 Kč, plus 25 Kč per kilometre after that. A reputable company is AAA Taxi, tel: 140 14.

CUSTOMS
The Czech customs controls have been greatly relaxed since accesson to the EU. Note that antiques more than 50 years old can only be taken out with a special permit, which can be very difficult to obtain.

CSA (CZECH AIRLINES)
See www.czechairlines.com
United Kingdom: Sovereign House, 361 King Street, Hammersmith, London W6 9NA; tel: 0870-444 3747.
United States: 1350 Avenue of the Americas, suite 601, New York 10019-4702; tel: 800-223 2365.
In Prague: Tickets and reservations: V Celnici 5, Prague 1, located near the Metro station Náměstí republiky. Flight information and reservations, tel: 239 007 007. Ruzyně Airport, Central information desk, tel: 220 111 111; www.csl.cz

TOURIST INFORMATION
The **Czech Centres** (www.czechcentres.cz) can provide a wealth of information. Also contact the local offices of **Czech Tourism** (www.czechtourism.com).
In the UK: The **Czech Centre**, 13 Harley Street, London W1G 9QG; tel: 020-7307 5180. **Czech Tourism**, Morley House, 320 Regent Street, W1B 3BG; tel: 020-7631 0427.
In the US: The **Czech Center**, 1109 Madison Avenue, New York, NY 10028; tel: 212-288 0830.
In Prague: The **Czech Tourist Authority** has an information centre at Vinohradska 46.
Around Prague Tourist Information (www.aroundprague.com) has centres at: Celetná 14, Prague 1, tel: 224 491 722; Karlova 1, Prague 1, tel: 221 663 105; Národní 4, Prague 1, tel: 224 901 160; Nerudova 4, Prague 1, tel: 257 535 123

Also very helpful is the **Prague Information Service** (PIS; www.pis.cz), located at Staroměstské náměstí (Old

Town Hall), Staré Město, tel: 12 444; at Na příkopě 20; and at the main (Wilsonova) railway station.

TRAVEL AGENCIES

CEDOK, the former state-run travel agency, now private, arranges all types of accommodation, as well as complete holidays to Prague and other destinations within the Czech Republic.
In the UK: Morley House, 314–322 Regent St, London, W1B 3BG, tel: 020-7580 3778; www.cedok.co.uk
In Prague: Na příkopě 18, tel: 224 197 632; Václavské náměstí 53, tel: 221 965 243; Rytiřská 16, tel: 224 224 461; www.cedok.cz

CURRENCY AND EXCHANGE

The national unit of currency is the Czech crown (koruna), for which the abbreviation is Kč. It is subdivided into 100 halér, abbreviated to h. Coins are in circulation to the value of 50 halér and 1, 2, 5, 10, 20 and 50 crowns. Banknotes are issued to the value of 20, 50, 100, 200, 500, 1,000, 2,000 and 5,000 crowns.

Exchange offices are often open during the evening and at weekends (especially those in the main railway station, in Václavské náměstí, Na příkopě and Staroměstské náměstí). Cash can also be obtained on credit/debit cards from 'Bancomat' ATM machines. International credit cards are now used widely.

SERVICE CHARGES AND TIPS

A service charge is included in bills issued by hotels and restaurants in Prague. An additional tip (about 10 percent of the total) is customary, depending on the standard of service.

OPENING TIMES

Shops are usually open Monday to Friday from 8.30am–6pm (sometimes with a midday break), and on Satur-

day until noon. An increasing number of shops in Prague open on Thursday until 8pm as well as on Saturday and Sunday afternoon.

Shops in the centre, selling goods of particular interest to tourists, often remain open until late in the evening in summer. Most museums are closed on Monday.

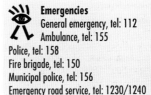

Emergencies
General emergency, tel: 112
Ambulance, tel: 155
Police, tel: 158
Fire brigade, tel: 150
Municipal police, tel: 156
Emergency road service, tel: 1230/1240
Lost and found office, tel: 224 235 085

POST

The main post office is near Václavské náměstí, at Jindřišská ul. 14. It is open 2am–midnight. Postboxes are orange.

TELEPHONE

It is usually easiest to make calls from a post office, as many public phones are on noisy streets. To make an international call, dial 00 + the international code: United Kingdom 44; US and Canada 1. Access numbers are: AT&T: 00-42-000-101; MCI: 00-42-000-112; Sprint: 00-42-087-187.

The code for the Czech Republic is 420. The Prague area code is 02 (omit the zero when calling from abroad). In the Czech Republic: Directory enquiries is 1180; International directory enquiries is 1181.

DIPLOMATIC REPRESENTATION

United Kingdom, Thunovská 14, Malá Strana; tel: 257 402 111; fax: 257 402 296; www.britain.cz
United States, Tržiště 15, Malá Strana; tel: 257 530 663; fax: 257 534 028; www.usembassy.cz

ACCOMMODATION

The tourist boom in Prague since 1989 at first overburdened the few hotels in the city centre, though the situation has now improved considerably. Accommodation is generally quite expensive – often on a par with Western Europe – and many hotels are booked up months in advance. It's always recommended to make a reservation. Many hotels can be found clustered around Wenceslas Square, although the most historic places to stay are in Hradčany and Malá Strana.

The hotels below are placed in three categories, for which the approximate prices in euros, per night in a double room, are as follows: **€€€** above €170; **€€** from €100 to €170; **€** below €100. Breakfast is usually included.

Hotel Selection

Hradčany and Malá Strana

Hotel Aria, Tržiště 9, tel: 225 334 111, www.ariahotel.net Expensive but chic, this new addition to Malá Strana plays heavily on its music theme. From Mozart to Dizzy Gillespie, each floor

Detail from the art nouveau Grand Hotel Europa (see page 83)

and room is dedicated to a particular music or musician. The fittings and fixtures are classy, as is the in-house music library. **€€€**

Hotel Neruda, Nerudova 44, tel: 257 535 557, www. hotelneruda.cz. A stone's throw away from the castle, this building dating from 1348 now has a minimalist modern interior. You are paying for the location as much as anything, but the rooms are clean and comfortable, and there is a pleasant café space where you can sit and sip hot chocolate. **€€€**

Hotel Savoy, Keplerova 6, tel: 224 302 430, www.hotel-savoy.cz. The Savoy offers luxury rooms, admittedly well done, of the kind found in many cities across the world. Perhaps it is this international familiarity that attracts the celebs, or, the stunning views across the Strahov Monastery and Petřín Hill from the Savoy and Presidential suites' balconies. **€€€**

U Červeného Lva, Nerudova 41, tel: 257 533 832, www.hotelredlion.com. A historic hotel set in a Renaissance house, previously the home of the baroque painter Peter Brandl. The rooms have wooden floors and beautifully painted ceilings; their views aren't bad either.

Under the hotel is a 14th century cellar, now a bar. €€€

Biskupský Dům, Dražického náměstí 6/62, tel: 257 532 320, www.hotelbishops house.com. Just off Mostecká, the 'Bishop's House' is a 19th century building close to the Charles Bridge. The somewhat plain rooms are clean and comfortable, and quiet, given the hotel's proximity to one of the city's main tourist thoroughfares. €€–€€€

Zlatá Hvězda, Nerudova 48, tel: 257 532 867, www.hotelgoldenstar.com. Perched looking down Nerudova and up to the castle, the 'Golden Star' has one of the best views of any hotel in the city. Dating back to 1372, the building's interior has been preserved and restored, and this careful approach has been carried over into the rooms, with their period furniture and modern bathrooms. €€–€€€

Dům u Velké Boty, Vlašská 30/333, tel: 257 532 088, www.dumuvelkeboty.cz Right opposite the German Embassy, and below the castle, this small hotel is in a superb location. The building dates from the early 17th century and care has been taken to ensure that the interior and furniture maintain the historic feel; thankfully with taste and restraint. Lovely comfy beds, spotless bathrooms and friendly owners all go towards making this one of the best places to stay in the city. €€

U Krále Karla, Nerudova/Úvoz 4, tel: 257 531 211, www.romantichotels.cz. This baroque building (it took its present form in 1639) is in a quiet and convenient location at the top of the hill, looking out over Petřín Hill. The rooms lean a little more towards Central European kitsch than some, but many people will enjoy the stained-glass windows. €€

U Modrého Klíče, Letenská 14, tel: 257 534 361, www.bluekey.cz. Just off the Lesser Quarter Square is a large baroque building – 'the Blue Key' –

now a hotel. The somewhat impersonal rooms are large and clean, and the location is convenient, if you don't mind the trams rattling past at regular intervals. A number of the rooms have a small cooker and fridge. €€

U Páva, U lužického semináře 32, tel: 257 533 360, www.romantichotels.cz. In a quiet location close to the Charles Bridge and not far from Kampa Island, this hotel has the same owners as U Krále Karla (above), and consequently has the same somewhat charming lean towards kitsch. The rooms have a nicely opulent feel to them, some with views of the castle. €€

Staré Město and Nové Město

Hotel Josef, Rybná 20, tel: 221 700 111, www.hoteljosef.com. A sleek designer hotel found near the Jewish Quarter. The modern interior, designed by Eva Jiricna, features stone and glass bathrooms attached to minimalist rooms (some of which are non-smoking) with dvd and cd players. None of this is cheap (up to around €350), but it does make a change from the often heritage-heavy accommo-dation available elsewhere in the city. €€€

Hotel Palace, Panská 12, tel: 224 093 111, www.palacehotel.cz. A Secessionist landmark, built in 1909 as a luxury hotel. It still performs this function today, though now it is only the facade that retains its art nouveau appearance. The interior was gutted in the 1980s to make way for comfortable, if a little impersonal, modern rooms. However, this apparent act of vandalism is off-set by excellent service. €€€

Hotel Paříž, Obecního domu 1, tel: 222 195 195 www.hotel-pariz.cz. More luxury in this squeaky-clean art nouveau building dating from 1904. Unfortunately the rooms have been rather over-restored and the original furniture replaced with bland modern pieces that make a nod in the direction of the original style. The restaurant Sarah Bernhardt has fared rather better and retains its sparkling interior and wooden fittings. €€€

Hotel Elite, Ostrovní 32, tel: 224 932 250, www.hotelelite.cz. Not many hotels in the New Town have a suite protected by the municipality, but Elite has, due to its impressive 17th century painted ceiling. The other rooms have also been tastefully preserved, with wooden floors, period furniture and an uncluttered feel. There is also a pleasant courtyard bar and café for the summer, and the Ultramarin restaurant. €€–€€€

Apostolic Residence, Staroměsteké náměstí 26, tel: 221 632 222, www.prague-residence.cz. Locations in the Old Town don't come much better than this tiny hotel right on the Old Town Square. The charming rooms with their wooden beams and period furniture may be a little more noisy than some – on the square and above a restaurant – but they do have a view of Astronomical Clock. €€

Hotel Axa, Na poříčí 40, tel: 224 812 580, www.hotelaxa.com. A long-established hotel in a modernist building close to the Old Town, the Axa has simple but clean and comfortable rooms at good prices considering its location. Its proudest features are the fitness centre and pool. €€

Hotel Opera, Těšnov 13, tel: 222 315 609, www.hotel-opera.cz. The impressive exterior of the 19th century hotel doesn't quite match up inside. However, the renovated rooms are pleasant and comfortable. Its central location and reasonable cost add considerably to its attractions. €€

U Tří Bubnů, U radnice 8/10, tel: 224 214 855, www.utribubnu.cz. The 'House at the Three Drums' can be found opposite Kafka's house, in the Old Town. In this small, newly converted residence you can choose between a room with an original painted wooden ceiling, one where the attached bathroom has a glass roof, or the two-storey attic apartment. €€

Pension Museum, Mezibranská 15, tel: 296 325 186, www.pension-museum.cz. This pension just off Wenceslas Square is well kept with a nice garden. Modern with wooden floors, the large and airy rooms are ideal for those with families, and the reasonable price includes a hearty buffet breakfast. €–€€

Pension Unitas, Bartolomějská 9, tel: 224 221 802, www.unitas.cz. There is a surprisingly homey feel to this cheap and clean hostel, considering it was used as a prison where Václav Havel was held during the 1970s (call ahead to reserve his room). The old cells have bunk beds and there are a few rooms with twin beds. Excellent value considering its central location and the inclusive buffet breakfast. €

Travellers' Hostels, Dlouhá 33, tel: 224 826 662, www.travellers.cz. This chain of hostels has half a dozen centrally located outlets, all clean and all very good value. The main branches are at Dlouhá 33, open all year; the others are open during the summer only. €

Elsewhere

Hotel Praha, Sušická 20, Prague 6, tel: 224 343 305/6, www.htlpraha.cz Conveniently close to the airport, this Stalinist concrete monstrosity has managed to turn its previous incarnation as a place exclusively for apparatchiks to its advantage; there is a certain chic to its modernist bulk, large rooms and built-in security measures. Aside from these, there are garden terraces and excellent service. €€€

Pension Vyšehrad, Krokova 6, Vyšehrad, tel: 241 408 455, www.pension-vysehrad.cz. A quiet, friendly, family-run pension with impressive views and a very attractive garden. There are only four simple but comfortable rooms, and a small dining room with a patio. Dogs and cats are welcome. €

INDEX